CERAMIC SKILLBOOKS

Series Editor:
Murray Fieldhouse

Working with
Porcelain

Alison Sandeman

PITMAN/WATSON-GUPTILL

PITMAN PUBLISHING LIMITED
39 Parker Street, London WC2B 5PB

Associated Companies
Copp Clark Limited, Toronto
Pitman Publishing New Zealand Ltd, Wellington
Pitman Publishing Pty Ltd, Melbourne

First published in Great Britain by Pitman Publishing Ltd 1979
Published in the USA by Watson-Guptill Publications 1979

© Pitman Publishing 1979

WATSON-GUPTILL PUBLICATIONS
a division of Billboard Publications Inc.,
1515 Broadway, New York, NY 10036

UK ISBN 0 273 01099 9 (cased edition)
UK ISBN 0 273 01112 X (paperback edition)
US ISBN 0-8230-5869-7

Text set in 10/12 pt IBM Century, printed by photolithography, and
bound in Great Britain at The Pitman Press, Bath

Contents

Acknowledgments

This book has been written with the help of many people. Thanks to my friend Sue Barker for much help and encouragement. I am especially indebted to David Leach for his advice and help. Thanks also to all the potters who gave their time and information so generously: Audrey Blackman, Sheila and Michael Casson, Janet Leach, Bill Marshall, Colin Pearson, Mary Rich, Marianne de Trey, Peter Simpson and Nigel Wood.

Thanks too to Biddy Woods for the illustrations and to Paul Wilson, Edward Piper and Peter Kinnear for the photographs. I am grateful to English China Clays Ltd, Emmanuel Cooper and Mary Rogers for supplying photographs. Also to The Fulham Pottery Ltd, Harrison Mayer Ltd, Potclays Ltd, Podmore and Son Ltd and English China Clays Ltd, for information about their products.

Finally thanks to my editor, David Lewis, for being so understanding and to all friends, family and potters for their encouragement.

Introduction

Although porcelain is a difficult clay body to work with, it can become easier to control with practice. The fineness of the body and the fired qualities of translucency, brightness and purity make porcelain more versatile and exciting than any other clay.

Like any clay, porcelain demands respect, patience, understanding and technical knowledge of its properties. This means more work and effort than usual by the potter before it can be mastered. But if it was the only clay, then all potters would have to work an 'apprenticeship' in porcelain before being able to use it to its fullest extent.

I hope this book will give practical help and encouragement to those who are new to porcelain but already familiar with other clays.

Fig. 1 Vase of Kinuta 'mallet' form. Porcelain with celadon glaze, Lung-ch'üan ware, Chinese 12th–13th century.
Victoria and Albert Museum

6

1 A Brief History of Porcelain

Fired porcelain is dense, white, vitrified and translucent where thin. It is made from a smooth, white body. Since stoneware is also dense, hard and fired to approximately the same high temperatures, porcelain can be described as a fine white translucent stoneware. The dividing line between porcelain and stoneware is often rather fine. However, porcelain has a higher degree of vitrification than stoneware, and glazes on porcelain combine more with the body. Potters tend to disagree on the correct firing temperatures for porcelain. A flexible attitude is best, since the materials used in a body will determine the firing temperature. Most potters fire their porcelain to 1280°C–1300°C, some fire higher. One of the commercial porcelain bodies is translucent at 1260°C–1280°C.

The origins of porcelain go back to the Chinese Han Dynasty (206 BC–AD 220) when a porcellanous stoneware body was produced. This slowly developed through to the translucent porcelains of the Tang (AD 618–906) and Sung Dynasties (AD 960–1279). Korean porcelain developed during the same period, while the Japanese learnt the techniques of porcelain making from the Chinese and the Koreans during the sixteenth and early seventeenth centuries.

The Chinese refer to all porcelain as 't'zu', a broad definition meaning that a vitrified pot made from any clay will give a distinctive ring when struck, whether translucent or not. In the West we attach much more importance to translucency, this being one of porcelain's most sought after qualities. To be translucent the ware must be thin enough to let light pass through. A translucent pot held up to daylight or a light bulb

Fig. 2 Small dish diameter 11 cm.
Porcelain with Ch'ing-pai glaze.
Chinese Sung Dynasty 12th—13th
century.
Victoria and Albert Museum

Fig. 3 Stem-cup. 14th century porcelain with a celadon glaze. Chinese, Lung-ch'üan from Chekiang province. Height 11.5 cm, diameter 12.5 cm.
Victoria and Albert Museum

will show the shadows of fingers behind. It is worth remembering that a thick porcelain pot, not obviously translucent, still has light passing through it, giving the pot the unique quality of porcelain that is difficult to describe but appreciated by potters and non-potters alike.

The qualities are closely related to the material itself. Chinese porcelain was made from just two materials, kaolin, a white clay, and petuntse, a natural mixture of potash mica, soda feldspar and quartz. Their nearest equivalents in the West are china clay and Cornish stone. The materials used and fired results of oriental porcelains are considerably different from those of the West. The name kaolin, incidentally, comes from the Chinese 'Kao' (high) and 'Ling' (hill, i.e. a high hill or ridge where the clay was first discovered).

There are two main reasons why it is not practical to create a porcelain body simply from china clay and Cornish stone. The Chinese kaolins are very plastic clays due to their small particle size. China clays in the West have a larger particle size and are not very plastic, so bentonite or ball clay has to be added to aid plasticity. Lack of silica is the other reason. The Chinese ingredients contain enough silica between them, whereas, with our Western porcelain bodies we have to add more silica in the form of quartz or flint to prevent porcelain glazes from crazing.

The word porcelain was probably derived from the Portuguese *porcellana*, the name of a translucent shell. Portuguese traders were one of the principal agents in the introduction of porcelain into more general use in Europe in the sixteenth century. At that time pottery in Europe was made of earthenware — soft, porous and often coarse. The imported porcelain excited wonder and amazement, being all that earthenware was not and could never be. Yet porcelain too was made from clay! The attempts to reproduce porcelain took place with fervent secrecy, and without success until 1710 when J. F. Böttger produced a true porcelain at Meissen. Many substitutes were also made which looked like porcelain but which were neither hard nor translucent, being basically white earthenware. These imitations of porcelain, known as soft paste, were fired to around 1100°C. Hard paste, true porcelain, using Western materials had to be fired to 1350—1450°C, to achieve the porcelain qualities using just china clay and Cornish stone or feldspar

The first English hard paste was made by William Cookworthy

who discovered the essential materials, china clay and Cornish stone, in the west country in 1768. His production of hard paste porcelain did not last long, however, due to technical difficulties. English porcelain manufacture continued with the soft paste bodies and bone china which was developed between 1750 and 1800. Bone china is a cross between soft paste and true porcelain and contains around 50 per cent bone ash (calcined bones). The use of bone ash as a body flux, meant that a translucent vitrified ware was possible at lower temperatures. Biscuit fired at 1250°C and glaze fired at 1080°C.

The history and techniques of porcelain making in China and the West are subjects well worth detailed study. Information can be found in many books and articles, some of which are listed in the Bibliography on page 92. What concerns us most in this volume, however, is porcelain as used by craft potters today.

British craft potters began to use a porcelain body largely through the influence of Bernard Leach, although technically speaking it was at first a porcellanous stoneware, that is, a smooth body compounded of china clay, ball clay, sometimes a feldspar, sometimes a grog. It was more like a white earthenware body taken up to stoneware and porcelain temperatures.

Bernard Leach was not concerned with translucency. His porcelain pots, although different to the thin, translucent work of others, express the same qualities of quietness, simplicity and strength of the Chinese Sung and Korean Ri Dynasty porcelains. It was these porcelains that influenced him so much. In *A Potter's Book* Bernard Leach tells us 'If we lay great stress upon Sung pottery it is not because we shall be content merely to imitate it but because it offers the highest and most universal standard with which to vitalize the technical achievements of the West.' Through Leach, more potters gradually began to use porcelain, at first in a small way, treating the material with great respect.

Bernard Leach's son, David, during his last years at the St Ives Pottery, 1951—55, became increasingly interested in developing a porcelain body that could be thrown thin and be translucent. Using the technical knowledge he had gained at the North Staffordshire Technical College, Stoke-on-Trent, 1934—37, he spent much time researching for a white, plastic translucent body. Considerable help came from the chemist, Edward Burke, and together they developed many complicated recipes for porcelain

Fig. 4 Bottle by Bernard Leach.
Photograph by Sue Barker

11

Fig. 5 (*opposite*) Decorated jar by
Bernard Leach
Photograph by Peter Kinnear

Fig. 6 (*above*) Porcelain coffee set
with oxide wash by Lucie Rie, 1956.
Photograph: Pottery Quarterly

Fig. 7 (*far left*) Bottle vase by Bill
Marshall, 1976.
Photograph by Sue Barker

Fig. 8 Teapot by Sheila Casson
made with the Podmore's David
Leach Porcelain Body.
Photograph by Sue Barker

bodies. Edward Burke introduced David Leach to various materials including the Quest White Bentonite, necessary for a plastic body. David Leach eventually simplified the recipes down to one, which he used successfully. This recipe not only formed the basis of the commercially produced 'David Leach body' by Podmore and Sons Ltd but it is also the recipe used most by potters who make up their own bodies. Some may use more or less quartz or a different bentonite. It is a logical recipe for the qualities required of a porcelain body, using the materials available to potters in the West.

Fig. 9 Lidded box by Bernard Leach. Decorated with oriental scenes in blue. 1912—13.
Photograph by Peter Kinnear

2 Porcelain Bodies

Working out a good porcelain body takes time, patience and the will to experiment. The process of research, experimenting, understanding the materials and testing out bodies is absorbing.

The main materials used in making up a porcelain body are china clay, feldspar and quartz. To make the body plastic the addition of bentonite or ball clay is necessary. Some knowledge of the geological background of the ingredients and the reasons for their use, will help in understanding their nature. Firing each material separately, as fusion buttons, will also reveal some of its characteristics. A further development would be to test the materials mixed together in various proportions. For example, 50 per cent china clay and 50 per cent feldspar or 75 per cent china clay and 25 per cent feldspar. This will help you to understand what happens to the materials when heated.

China clay $Al_2O_3 . 2SiO_2 . 2H_2O$

The clay content of a porcelain body comes from china clay, a primary clay found mainly in Cornwall (England), Georgia, South Carolina and Florida (USA), Germany, France and Czechoslovakia. China clay is the result of the hydrothermal decomposition of feldspars in granite. This chemical process caused by heated water and hot acidic gases underground, rather than by weathering above ground, is called kaolinization and results in kaolinite. Kaolinite is the clay mineral of china clay or kaolin.

The degree of plasticity of a clay depends on its particle size. The smaller the particle size, the more plastic it will be. China clay has a particle size at least ten times larger than that of a plastic ball clay, and is therefore not very plastic. It is a very pure, white burning and refractory clay with a large particle size and low shrinkage.

There are, however, many different types of china clay, some more plastic than others. For purity it is important to select one that has a low iron content. Clay companies will supply technical data sheets that show chemical analyses including iron content. Standard Porcelain, Grolleg and Treviscoe from English China Clays Ltd, are the china clays favoured by most British potters who make up their own porcelain. These are also available in the US along with Georgia kaolin and EPK. English China's Standard

Fig. 10 A general view of the West Carclaze china clay pit.
Photograph: English China Clays Group

Porcelain China Clay and China Clay No 50 from Watts, Blake, Bearne and Co Ltd, are about the best available to British potters. They have a finer particle size than other china clays, which aids plasticity and gives bodies good dry strength. In the US individual suppliers offer their own porcelain mixtures (refer to US Suppliers' List on page 90).

The china clay from Cornwall is extracted by playing high pressure, remotely-controlled water hoses, known as monitors, on to the rock face of kaolinized granite (see Fig. 11). This washes out the clay and mica which flow to the bottom of the pit. They are then pumped to a sand separation plant where coarse quartz sand is extracted. The settled slurry is pumped out of the pit to

Fig. 11 A remote-controlled power hose or monitor washing raw clay from the pit face.
Photograph: English China Clays Group

cyclone separators where the mica is separated out. After this the clay is thickened, dried out and crushed to a fine powder. The waste coarse sand and mica form the familiar white hills around the St Austell district in Cornwall.

Feldspar $K_2O.Al_2O_3.6SiO_2$ (Potash feldspar)

Decomposed from granite and igneous rocks, feldspar has a melting point of around $1200°C$, and is the body flux in a porcelain body. The melting of feldspar is sluggish, allowing vitrification to happen at an even rate. A material such as talc, which contains the flux magnesium, melts far quicker and would cause collapse. Molten feldspar has a high viscosity which helps a porcelain body to resist alteration during firing and also contributes to the translucency of the body without collapse. However, if used in excess or fired too high, feldspar is a material that will cause collapse. Feldspar is fairly free from iron contamination so adds to the purity of a body but it is a non-plastic material. Potash feldspar is to be preferred since it has a more viscous melt than soda feldspar. Cornish stone can be used instead but this will raise the maturing temperature of a body. Some of the potash feldspar can be substituted by nepheline syenite to lower the maturing temperature of a body.

Silica SiO_2 (Quartz)

As china clay and feldspar do not contain enough silica between them it is necessary to add quartz or flint. Silica gives strength, hardness and purity to a body. Quartz is purer than flint, but flint does have a finer particle size and therefore converts more easily to cristobalite. Most potters use waterground quartz or finely ground flint. The addition of quartz or flint to a body helps to stop glazes crazing but an excess of twenty five per cent of it can cause cracking in a body. The grain size of quartz or flint is important, as explained on page 20.

Ball clay

As sedimentary clays ball clays have a very fine particle size, they are therefore highly plastic. They usually contain impurities, including iron and titanium, gathered during their geological transportation. It is necessary to select as white burning a ball clay as possible, but it is accepted that in gaining plasticity, some purity of the fired clay will be lost. Ball clay porcelains tend to fire grey. Test ball clays as fusion buttons to establish their degree of purity. The ball clays of Devon and Dorset in the west of England are reasonably pure but as the Dorset clays were transported and deposited further from their parent rocks they are less pure. In the United States ball clays should be sought that are lowest in iron content, such as Kentucky ball clay # 4.

Ball clays vitrify at low temperatures and they add strength to raw ware, which aids handling. A high proportion of china clay in a body can make biscuit pots crumbly and chalky. Ball clay gives strength at this stage too.

Many potters will argue that a porcelain body containing ball clay is not a true porcelain. However it is possible to obtain a translucent body, fired to 1280°C, containing 25 per cent ball clay.

Bentonite

Bentonite comes from the montmorillonite group of clay minerals. It is a natural clay of very fine particle size and has 'super plasticity'. Only small amounts can be used for the following reasons: most bentonites contain iron which will discolour the fired clay, though it is possible to obtain white burning bentonite. Bentonite has a high shrinkage due to its small colloidal particle size. Besides this, the high proportion of silica in bentonite can cause shattering of the body in the glaze firing, due to the release of free silica. The use of bentonite can cause problems in turning and firing (see pages 60 and 80). Sodium bentonite swells as it takes up water, so it is advisable to use calcium bentonite. Up to 5 per cent bentonite is usual in a porcelain body. Quest White and Berkonite are good white burning bentonites but they are not always available. In the US often only one kind of bentonite is available.

Cobalt

Very small quantities of cobalt are sometimes added to give a body artificial whiteness. To avoid speckling it should be passed through a 200 mesh sieve.

What happens to porcelain in firing

During firing, porcelain bodies start to vitrify. The clay particles are drawn together (shrinkage) and any pores are filled in by a glassy bond. Vitrification is the process of fluxes fusing the clay particles together, creating a glassy mass. Potassium oxide (K_2O) in potash feldspar is the flux which starts to melt at around 1160°C, then slowly combines with and dissolves the china clay and silica. This viscous liquid dissolves the silica into silica glass (fused silica) and free silica. The combination of feldspar, china clay and silica glass forms the vitrified, translucent body. The free silica is converted slowly to cristobalite and what remains is known as free quartz.

The thermal expansion of a body is determined by the amount of cristobalite and free quartz. On cooling, the body contracts. If there is too much cristobalite and free quartz there will be a loss of vitrification and translucency. This is because not enough silica has been converted to silica glass. An excess of free quartz and cristobalite will cause high shrinkage and result in the body shivering, spiral-cracking or shattering. However, there is little danger of this happening with a standard porcelain recipe. If there is not enough cristobalite and free quartz in the body then glazes may craze. During cooling the free quartz shrinks at 575°C and the cristobalite at 220°C. These shrinkages put the body into a state of compression and help to prevent crazing (see page 67).

The particle size of quartz and the length of firing determine the amount of quartz that is converted to silica glass and therefore the degree of vitrification and translucency. The silica in china clay and feldspar converts to silica glass easier than quartz, as the particle size is finer. The finer the particle size the more surface area there is for the fluxes to work on, converting silica into silica glass. The larger particle size of added quartz needs a long firing. This allows more time for the particles to be dissolved into silica glass. The more undissolved silica left in a body the less translucent it will be. For this reason porcelain bodies benefit from a long soak towards the later stages of firing (see page 79).

Proportions and recipes

Having observed how the materials fire on their own and in combination, recipes can be formulated. Remember that the qualities of purity, whiteness and translucency will not only be affected by the different proportions and quality of materials, but also by the kiln atmosphere and temperature (see Chapter 6).

The following is a good base from which potters can develop a recipe for their own particular needs. (Note to American potters: flint can be substituted for quartz throughout.)

1   China clay   50
    Potash feldspar 25
    Quartz   25

N.B. Either bentonite or ball clay must be added to this basic recipe to give plasticity.

It will help at this point to give an idea of the possible maximum quantities of each material in a body.

China clay   Around 50 per cent is usual.

Potash feldspar   Less than 25 per cent will result in a loss of translucency if firing temperatures are 1250—1280°C. This percentage can be reduced to around 18 per cent if the firing temperature is higher. More than 25 per cent could lead to collapse of the body.

Quartz   Less than 15 per cent quartz (silica) will impede glaze fit, causing crazing. More than 25 per cent can cause shattering.

Bentonite   Around 5 per cent is usual. Some potters use 6 per cent, other potters consider 2—3 per cent plenty.

Ball clay   Around 10 per cent is ideal for colour, but not enough for plasticity. 15 per cent is a good figure. Maximum 25 per cent. Experiment with say, 10 per cent ball clay and 1 per cent bentonite.

2   China clay   50   The ball clay can be increased
    Potash feldspar 25   to 15 per cent and the china
    Quartz   15   clay reduced to 45 per cent.
    Ball clay   10

Using bentonite for plasticity the quartz can be increased to 20 per cent, and there will be less chance of glazes crazing. 5 per cent bentonite is about the maximum that should be used. Experiment with 2—3 per cent.

3	China clay	50
	Potash feldspar	25
	Quartz	20
	Bentonite	5

The recipe above is a good one and is only a step away from David Leach's recipe:

4	Grolleg China Clay	53
	Potash feldspar	25
	Waterground quartz	17
	Bentonite	5

The following recipe contains 25 per cent ball clay and makes a good throwing body which is translucent at $1280°C$. Some purity will be lost using such a large quantity of ball clay, giving a grey fired colour.

5	China clay	25
	Potash feldspar	25
	Quartz	25
	Ball clay	25

Note the low amount of china clay. The clay content is divided equally between china clay and ball clay.

Using these recipes as a basis the potter can experiment by preparing small amounts, testing out and adjusting the proportions if necessary. For example, recipe 5 has a high percentage of ball clay. The ball and china clays could be adjusted leaving the feldspar and quartz the same. This will give a whiter but less plastic body.

6	China clay	35
	Potash feldspar	25
	Quartz	15
	Ball clay	15

In general the bentonite porcelains are best. Good plasticity can be achieved using 5 per cent. This leaves china clay at around 50 per cent, necessary for a white body.

Recipe 3 gives excellent results, using Standard Porcelain china clay fired in our oil kiln to $1280°C$, reduction atmosphere. It also works well in an oxidizing atmosphere. However, some glazes crazed on this body and we found better results could be achieved with the following recipe:

7   Standard Porcelain china clay 45
    Potash feldspar   25
    Waterground quartz   25
    Bentonite   5

Individual requirements will control proportions and firing
temperatures. Careful consideration must be given to the qualities
required in a porcelain body. One potter may be satisfied with a
good, plastic body that is comparatively easy to work with but
which lacks good translucency and a very white body. Translucency and whiteness may mean a loss of plasticity and the
potter will need to develop patience and skill in handling an
excellent clay, low in plasticity.

Any iron oxide present in ball clay or bentonite will come out
in a reducing atmosphere as iron specks. However, the occasional
iron specks may be compensated for by the superb glaze
qualities that can be achieved on porcelain in a reduction kiln.
(Equally fine glazes can, of course, be achieved in an oxidizing
kiln.)

Changing a body recipe

In his *Pottery Quarterly* articles on porcelain, John Reeve
explained how he had to change his porcelain body. His first
porcelain body was fired to cone 10 with a long soaking period
above cone 8. The results were good and the glazes did not craze.

Grolleg china clay 56   Quartz   14
Potash feldspar   28   Bentonite   2

However, when he fired the same body in kilns with a short
firing cycle he found that the glazes crazed. The quick firing did
not give enough time for the formation of cristobalite. Reeve
spent months testing, before he learned that his friend Warren
MacKenzie had experienced the same problems with roughly
the same body and solved them by *doubling* the silica content!
With more silica in the body there was more cristobalite and free
quartz to prevent crazing. When Reeve almost doubled the quartz
in his body, the crazing stopped.

China clay 45   Quartz   26
Feldspar   17   Bentonite   6

Making up porcelain bodies

With careful planning porcelain bodies can easily be made up in quantities of around 2 cwt. Most potters will probably find that 1 cwt is sufficient to make up in one go, since so little is used unless you are going in for full scale production! Test batches are usually made up in small quantities of 5 lbs or less.

Two methods suitable for the preparation of bodies are described below, one for potters with no mechanical equipment and the other for those with blunger or ball mill, filter press and pug mill. Whichever method is used, all equipment must be clean. Plastic, wood or even pottery containers are preferable to metal ones which may rust and contaminate the clay. For the preparation and use of porcelain on a large scale a separate room is ideal.

While most potters use ready-powdered china clay, feldspar, quartz and bentonite or ball clay, those who are adventurous enough to want to dig their own materials will find Michael Cardew's *Pioneer Pottery* extremely helpful. An important point that Michael Cardew makes in this book is that china clay will lose a lot of its plasticity if added as a dry powder to the other materials. Always add china clay as a thin slip to the rest already in slip form.

Hand mixing

Having weighed out the powdered feldspar, quartz and bentonite or ball clay, thoroughly dry mix them and then sprinkle the mix slowly into a container of water. As a rough guide, 3 lbs of dry materials will require approximately 3 pints of water. Leave this mixture to soak for at least 24 hours allowing the materials to become saturated with water. Add the china clay to a separate container of water to make a thin slip. Note that the bentonite is mixed in dry with the feldspar and quartz. Bentonite added to water on its own gathers up into globules and becomes quite unmanageable. After 24 hours, drain off any excess water from the feldspar, quartz, bentonite or ball clay mixture, hand stir for about five minutes, and then put through a 100 mesh sieve. Hand stir the china clay slip, including the excess water that will have settled on top, then add to the rest, stirring at the same time if possible. The complete mixture should then be put through a 100 mesh sieve. If it is a very thin mix it may be necessary to dewater it by pouring it into canvas trays (see Fig. 12) or canvas

Fig. 12 Wood and canvas tray for dewatering very liquid clay.

bags. The water will slowly drip through the canvas and this thickening up may take two or three days. Once thickened it can be put out on to plaster or wooden bats, or absorbent tiles to stiffen up to the plastic usable state.

If the slip is thick enough after sieving there is no need for this rather elaborate process. In our own pottery I usually put the slip straight on to plaster bats from the bucket after sieving. When stiffening up the clay, avoid the formation of a hard outer layer, as soft and hard lumps in porcelain do not mix together well. If plaster bats are used, a hard layer may form next to the plaster. To avoid this, dampen the bat slightly before use. With other drying methods a hard layer may form on top, particularly in a warm atmosphere. A damp cloth over the clay will stay damp as water evaporation and filtration take place, preventing a hard crust forming.

Mechanical mixing
Porcelain can also be made up with the use of a blunger or ball mill. Blunging in a ball mill for three to four hours is especially recommended for dispersing water amongst the materials. As described above, dry mix the materials, reduce to a slip and add the china clay to the rest as a thin slip. Blunging can then take place immediately although it is a good idea to leave the materials to soak in water for a few hours. After blunging, dewatering and stiffening up can take place, as already described, although if porcelain is being made on a fairly large scale a filter press is useful. After stiffening, the clay can be passed through the pug mill. Clean out the pug mill thoroughly before use and watch out for rusty particles in an old machine. It is best to pug the clay only once, as over pugging can cause loss of plasticity.

Wedging and kneading for storage

The preparation of a porcelain body should not be hurried. Care, cleanliness and time taken during the making up process will increase workability and plasticity.

Once the clay has stiffened up to the plastic condition required for hand-building or throwing, wedge or knead and then wrap in clean polythene for storage and ageing in a damp or cool place. It is usual to store porcelain slightly softer than required for use as, like any clay, it will slowly harden.

A porcelain body should be aged for at least six months to develop the qualities of plasticity and workability. A year is better still. Many potters find up to two years necessary for their requirements while others, eager to try out the new clay, may find a few weeks sufficient. Try the clay out at various times during the ageing process, say once a month, and a knowledge and appreciation of the clay will develop.

Damp rags or old clothes wrapped round the clay and then covered with polythene will help to develop the bacterial action. Leave damp rags next to the clay for short periods only. Removing a rotting towel from porcelain that has been ageing for five years can be very frustrating — though the clay itself may be beautiful to use! Discovering an old packet of porcelain in a cluttered pottery must be like discovering a case of vintage wine. Vinegar, incidentally, can be added to develop and hurry the ageing process, and although the smell is not to be recommended, it does disappear eventually.

Making up batches of porcelain well in advance is important and advantageous. Chinese porcelain was sometimes prepared by one generation for use by the next.

Testing new bodies

It should be noted that small tests will only give a limited indication of qualities and faults: it may not be until a fair quantity of porcelain is fired that a true assessment of quality can be made.

Test new porcelain bodies in the same way as other clays. Detailed records should be kept and the clay left to rest for at least a week before testing. A month is better for indications of plasticity. From storage knead the clay and make notes on the degree of plasticity and stickiness. Making small pinch pots will give further indications of plasticity and strength. Porcelain is usually thirsty to throw with, so observe water absorption.

For each body being tested make about eight test tiles 8 cm long, 4 cm wide and $\frac{1}{4}$ cm thick (3 x 2 x $\frac{1}{10}$ in.). They will be very fragile in the raw state. Mark one with a 5 cm (2 in.) line, as in Fig. 15, so that shrinkage measurements from plastic to dry, and plastic to fired state can be measured. Porcelains usually shrink about 16–17 per cent from plastic to fired state. From plastic to dry they usually shrink 10 per cent.

Fig. 13 (*left*) Testing for workability.
Left A short body. This can be
caused by lack of plastic material in
the body or lack of ageing. *Right* A
well-aged plastic body that pinches
thin without cracking.
Photograph by C Paul Wilson

Fig. 14 (*below*) David Leach kneading.
Photograph by Edward Piper

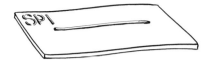

Fig. 15 Shrinkage test tile with 5 cm line incised.

Snap a dry tile in half to test for dry strength. A piece of clay can be pinched out as thin as possible to test for translucency. The $\frac{1}{4}$ cm thick tiles may also be translucent. The tiles will need turning once or twice to prevent warping while drying. Allow one tile to dry out without turning it over. This will indicate warpage from plastic to dry. Remember, though, that tiles always warp more than pots (see Fig. 16).

After biscuit firing measure the shrinkage tile and investigate another for general strength and any tendency to crumble. Test another for porosity by dipping it either into water or glaze.

Glaze fire the shrinkage tile and translucency piece unglazed. Test two tiles with glazes you know. Another tile placed on two refractory dots will indicate sagging and collapse. After the firing make notes on final shrinkage measurements, translucency, colour and texture of body, glaze fit, degree of vitrification and deformation. The thin piece held up to the light will show its translucency. A thicker piece may have to be held up to a light bulb. If a body gives indications of being a success after test tiles, test it further by making small pots.

Some faults

Distortion   If a body distorts badly, it may contain too much feldspar. Change the recipe by reducing the amount of feldspar. Bad setting or placing in the kiln can also cause pots to go out of shape. (See page 79 for firing faults.)

Body colour   If you are not satisfied with the fired body colour try changing the china clay or bentonite or ball clay. Bad body colour may indicate not enough china clay in the recipe.

Fig. 16 Raw tiles showing how five different bodies warp from plastic to dry.
Photograph by C Paul Wilson

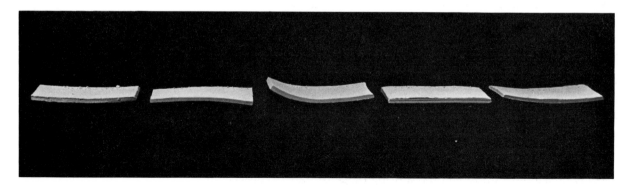

Vitrification   A body that does not vitrify enough probably contains too much china clay. Try reducing the china clay content.

Translucency   Loss of translucency is usually due to too much china clay or not enough feldspar. The degree of purity of the materials used can also affect translucency. A bentonite rather high in iron content will discolour the body and decrease translucency.

Glaze fit   See page 67 for notes on bad glaze fit.

When correcting any fault only change one material at a time in order to establish which material is giving trouble.

As porcelain should be fired from 1250°C onwards most potters can include porcelain tests in their normal firings. In general, firing to around 1280°C will give better results for tests. Those potters with the use of both electric and flame kilns could carry out extensive tests to discover the difference between oxidized and reduced porcelain. Both have their advantages. All the qualities and characteristics of porcelain will be affected differently, depending on kiln atmosphere.

Always test out more than one recipe at a time so that one result can be compared with another. In this way a working knowledge of porcelain bodies can be developed.

Commercially produced porcelain bodies

Potters with little time, space or equipment for making up their own body will find, on page 89, a Suppliers' List for commercially prepared bodies.

One of the most popular commercial bodies is the David Leach Porcelain Body from Podmore & Sons Ltd. Many well known potters use this very practical body for hand-building and throwing. It becomes translucent at 1260—1280°C, and is available in plastic or powdered form.

The code numbers printed on the clay packs indicate the week and year in which it was produced. This is most valuable in assessing how aged and plastic the clay may be. For example 30—7 indicates that the clay was produced in week 30 of 1977. This coding refers to Podmore's David Leach Body only and not to their other products.

The Harrison Mayer body is a semi-porcelain vitreous earthenware. It fires a pure white and has a firing range of 1200—1300°C but it is not translucent at their recommended firing temperature of 1220°C. At that temperature there is little problem of distortion. However, fired carefully to 1280°C it does become semi-translucent. The body is a blend of ball clay and china clay and it also contains barium carbonate, cobalt bleaching stain and a vegetable dye. Commercial bodies are often stained with a vegetable dye, which burns out in firing.

Potclays' Standard Porcelain Body also has a good fired colour and translucency. The recommended approximate firing temperature is 1280—1350°C, and it is available in plastic form.

The Fulham Pottery Porcelain Body also fires to a good colour, handles well and is translucent at 1280°C. It matures in the range 1240—1280°C.

Try a variety of commercially-prepared bodies and then use the one that works best for the type of work you do and the firing conditions available. Porcelain is becoming so popular that pottery suppliers are continually developing and improving their bodies

In the United States, Westwood Ceramic Supply Co. (see US Suppliers' List on page 90) offers two popular porcelain bodies, both of which mature at the cone 10 range: Keni porcelain for hand-building and Kai porcelain for throwing. These bodies are available through selected suppliers across the USA. Other than these, various ceramic suppliers offer their own mixes which should be tested by the potter in small quantities for suitability to his work. As in the UK, pottery suppliers are continually developing and improving their porcelain bodies.

3 Hand-building with Porcelain

Hand-building is one of the most exciting and satisfying ways of working with porcelain. In general a good workable plastic clay is necessary for pinching, folding, forming and pressing but it is possible to use a fairly short body for slab work.

Pinch pots

The ideal way to understand the nature of a porcelain body is by making pinch or thumb pots. This process of forming pots by hand is a good introduction for hand-builders and those who intend to use porcelain on the wheel. Pinch pots are best made slowly and carefully with fairly soft clay. Porcelain tends to dry out quicker than earthenware or stoneware, especially when being held in warm hands. With practice you soon become familiar with the nature of porcelain and pinching can be developed into a rewarding and satisfying technique.

The usual methods of forming pinch pots are used. As the thumb enters the ball of clay a slight resistance to formation may be noticed by those used to forming pinch pots with more plastic, open textured clays. Clay that is too soft will stick to thumb or fingers and tear. It will also cause a pot to flop and collapse before it is finished. It is always useful to have a small clean plaster bat handy for stiffening up small amounts of clay quickly. Clay that is too hard is very difficult to work. It will crack and crumble at the edges. If this happens, join the pot back to the main lump, cut it up into thin slices, like a loaf of bread, and leave it in a bowl of water for around ten minutes, or until it becomes soft. Then re-knead the clay. It may be possible to use the clay after this wetting down process or it may need a day or so to rest.

In general it is not wise to use water on a pinch pot during making as this creates a very sticky surface to work with. Fingers may stick to and tear the clay, which will become floppy. A pot that is going well and has had a lot of time spent on it may get to the stage of needing a little damping down. Handsprays, such as those used for gardening, or a mouthspray, usually used for fixing charcoal drawing, are useful for spraying water on to a pot. Remember that porcelain not only dries out quicker than other clays but it also absorbs water more easily and softens fairly quickly. This is due to the large particle size of china clay.

When first pinching porcelain, concentrate on getting the feel of the clay and do not worry about making pots to keep. Pinch as thin as possible, find out its limitations, learn about the clay. When pinching, the clay will naturally flare outwards. This tendency can be exploited for bowl shapes but it will be necessary to support them, see Figs. 19 and 20. Halfway through making a bowl or flare-shaped form it may need this support while it dries a little. This may only take half an hour or so in warm weather or artificial heat. After that the pot can be thinned out further but be careful not to allow cracks to develop.

It is best not to be too ambitious with your first pinch pots in porcelain. Very flared shapes can slump easily in the firing, so

Fig. 17 A good test for the workability of a body. Making pinch pots. pots. *Right* Cracking up of the clay indicates a short body or the clay may be too dry. *Left* A good plastic body.
Photograph by C Paul Wilson

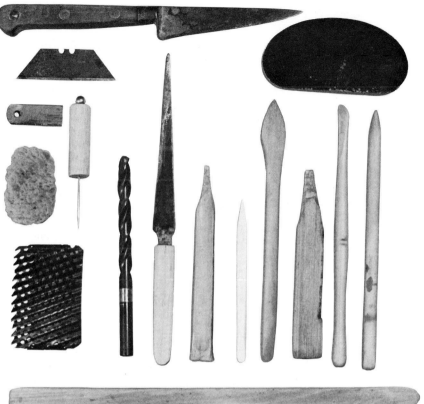

Fig. 19 Supporting a shape with paper.

Fig. 20 A delicate pinch pot can be supported with sponges while drying in a bowl.

slightly flaring bowls are good shapes to start on.

Closed-over or inward-going shapes are a little more difficult to make. Always keep a narrow opening, finish pinching the bottom section first and then develop the top half. The walls of the pot are pinched inwards all the time and by holding the pot in the hand the tendency to flare outwards is restricted.

Any cracks that do appear while pinching should be bonded together and smoothed over, using fingers or a modelling tool, before they get any worse. Potters often make use of accidents that happen during the forming process. The splitting of rims on pinch pots, for example, can be used as decoration by pinching the edges thinner and thus slightly exaggerating splits, as in Fig. 21. Asymmetry is inevitable and also acceptable in this kind of work, giving pinch pots a very different character to thrown work.

Fig. 21 Pinch-built bowl with
dapped interior by Mary Rogers.
*Reproduced by kind permission of
Ceramic Review*

If a foot-ring is required on a pot then it can be made in two
ways. It is possible to leave enough thickness at the bottom of
the pot to allow the pinching down of a foot-ring. This can leave
rather an irregular foot which can be trimmed with a sharp knife
at the leather hard stage. A better method is to join a foot-ring on.
Roll out a piece of clay, cut it into a strip, wrap it into a circle
and join the ends. This kind of foot-ring should be made at the
same time as the pot and then joined at the leather hard stage.
Score and add slurry to the surfaces to be joined. Allow the
slurry to dry a little and then join together. The slurry that
oozes out either side, if left to dry out to normal plastic consistency, can be used as reinforcement by smoothing it into the
joins with the fingers or modelling tool. A small roll of clay can
be attached to the outside or inside of the foot-ring for further
reinforcement, if necessary.

As a pot is being made the fingers will leave small impressions

Fig. 22 Pinch-built porcelain.
Tree-edged bowl by Mary Rogers.

Fig. 23 Open Spinner form by
Peter Simpson, 1975.
Victoria and Albert Museum

on the surface which can either be smoothed over or, if not too deep, can be left for the finishing off process. Just as throwing rings on a porcelain bowl would interrupt the flow of the form, so will finger marks on hand-built work. Finger marks left on a thin translucent piece will show up badly as dark and light patches. Always aim to leave as few irregularities on the surface as you can during the making process.

It is good to have two or three pots on the go at the same time. In this way one pot can be resting and stiffening up a little while work is started on another. This also introduces a rhythm to working, particularly desirable if a theme is being worked out.

Finishing can be carried out at the leather hard stage. Use a finely toothed hacksaw blade to scrape away bumps and irregularities on the outside. This will leave a finely combed surface which can be scraped smooth with the back of the blade, a metal kidney or razor blade. Alternatively the metal kidney or razor blade can be used from the beginning. Use a kidney or sharpened spoon for the inside if necessary. Many potters prefer to finish pots when they are completely dry, since there is a danger of distorting or cracking a piece at the leather hard stage. However a bone dry piece will be extremely fragile and should be scraped carefully with sharp metal tools. Always hold the piece in your hands. You will build up an intuitive feeling of how to handle dry pieces in their most vulnerable state.

Much of the finest hand-built porcelain made today is based on or directly influenced by natural forms. This can be clearly seen in Figs. 21 and 22. Nature offers us an unlimited supply of ideas. Many potters build up collections of seed pods, fruits, pebbles, grasses, shells, bones and fungi (see Fig. 24). Drawing is a good way to develop ideas from such a collection and to investigate form and clay. The shapes that work best are either developments or simplified versions of natural forms. Direct copies of shapes in nature never seem to work well in porcelain. Pinch pots joined together form good basic shapes that can have holes cut into them or be worked on in various ways.

Press-moulding

Press-moulded shapes can be used in conjunction with pinched work, particularly for more sculptural forms. Basic shapes can be formed in a plaster or biscuit mould and then developed by pinching the edges thin or pinched shapes can have press-moulded forms joined to them. Some potters cast the basic shapes with casting slip and then add to them.

Soft clay is used for press moulding as hard clay will crack easily during formation. For wide shallow internal moulds a single slice of clay, cut as in Fig. 26, can be laid in without creasing or folding. For narrow or deep moulds it is sometimes necessary to build up the walls with two or three pieces of clay, as a single piece would crease badly. Creases can be used as a form of decoration, but if they are not wanted they can be filled in with soft clay after release from the mould.

After clay is pressed into a mould it is trimmed with a sharp knife, allowed to dry for approximately ten minutes and then released. Avoid leaving clay in contact with plaster for too long as a hard outer crust may form and the clay may dry out too much for additions to be made. Leave the clay in the mould just long enough for it to become firm enough to handle without distortion.

Small press-moulded plates and dishes can be made with porcelain. For larger ones add a china clay grog such as Molochite as described in the section on slab building below. Press-moulded boxes are made with soft clay as the plaster dries the clay quickly and there is a tendency for the walls to keep pulling away from the mould. Very soft clay does not work well as it sticks to the fingers. Make the boxes fairly quickly and trim off the excess clay with a sharp knife. After the lid and box are released place the lid on the box and use a damp sponge to smooth over the leather hard bumps and irregularities, This works well on a smooth porcelain body. A light touch with the damp sponge will remove the sharp edges of flanges. Thick porcelain boxes are very enjoyable to make and handle, but thin sectioned boxes are best left to the slip casting technique.

Slab building

Thick slab pots in porcelain also work well. Like the press-moulded dishes and boxes they form an interesting contrast to thin, translucent pinch or thrown pots. To avoid warping, make slabs with fairly thick pieces of clay and if possible use a body

Fig. 24 Seedpods give ideas for forms.
Photograph by C Paul Wilson

with a fairly low shrinkage. Porcelain shrinks a lot from wet to dry and again in the glaze firing. If the slabs are kept flat when drying out to the leather hard state, the only warping that is likely to occur will be in the glaze firing, when the clay vitrifies.

Slabs can be cut from a block of clay as shown in Fig. 26. The block of clay should be at least 1.25 cm ($\frac{1}{2}$ in.) bigger all round than the required working measurements. This will allow for wet to leather hard shrinkage. The block can be placed on canvas or similar material to prevent sticking down. If working on a wooden table or chipboard (US particle board) move the block each time to prevent sticking down. Sticks of the required thickness of slabs are placed either side of the block. With thumbs firmly holding down a wire on the sticks a slab is cut through. The block is moved on and cutting continues. Chipboard (US particle board) is an ideal surface for drying out slabs. For even drying they may need turning once or twice. Dry

Fig. 25 Kneading in molochite in
the same way as grog is kneaded
into stoneware bodies.
Photograph by C Paul Wilson

them out to the leather hard state before cutting to the required
measurements. Remember when working out final measurements
for a slab pot that porcelain usually shrinks 16—17 per cent.

A fairly short body can be used for cutting slabs but a more
plastic one is needed for rolling out. For this the clay should be
soft to prevent cracking and a dry clean rolling pin used, otherwise clay will stick to it. Some potters roll porcelain out
between two pieces of material or polythene to prevent sticking.
Depending on the materials used, interesting textures can be
achieved. Thin polythene may introduce creases into the clay
which can form useful decoration. (Thick polythene will not
cause creases.)

For assembly, slabs should be leather hard. After slurry has
been applied to the scored edges, porcelain slabs sometimes
become limp as they absorb moisture from the wet slurry. After
assembly the slurry that has oozed out is left to dry to plastic

consistency and then smoothed in to form a bond on the inside joins. Excess slurry on the outside can be removed with a modelling tool. A surform blade can be used lightly to remove irregularities and then a damp sponge or sharp blade used to remove the surform blade marks. Sharp edges are rounded off with a sponge or finger tips.

Finished slab pots can be dried off naturally or, if cracking seems likely to occur, wrapped up in polythene for a couple of days to slow down the drying process.

Fig. 26 Cutting slabs from a block of clay. The molochite in the body gives an interesting texture and strength to the pot.
Photograph by C Paul Wilson

Molochite

Hand-built work using soft slabs is also possible with porcelain. It may be necessary to support pieces with wood, sponges or paper to avoid collapse as they dry. A good plastic body will fold and bend well. Try simple shapes at first while you are finding out what the clay will stand up to in the firing.

For larger work Molochite, a product of English China Clays Ltd, can be kneaded into the clay (see Fig. 25). Molochite is china clay that has been calcined, in the form of small bricks, to 1525°C.

Fig. 27 Assembly of slab pot. *Photograph by C Paul Wilson*

After calcining, the bricks are crushed to produce Molochite of various grades. Although produced for industry it is possible for potters to obtain it (see Suppliers' List). Since Molochite is a refractory grog it decreases shrinkage of a clay and is therefore extremely useful for large slab pots and pressed flat dishes in porcelain. It is used in roughly the same way as fireclay grog is added to stoneware and gives an interesting appearance to the surface of a pot. For dramatic effects use a large grade such as 'coarse $\frac{1}{4}$—8'. As the clay shrinks and dries the Molochite pieces are left sticking out slightly and if a large grade is used the clay splits a little round each piece. As a rough guide 8 oz of Molochite kneaded into 4 lb of clay seems to work well. Experiment with smaller or larger amounts. Fig. 27 shows the assembly of slabs made from a ball clay porcelain and coarse grade Molochite. Marianne de Trey uses old high temperature insulating bricks crushed up and passed through a 30's mesh sieve. This makes grog for some porcelain work.

Decorating hand-built pots

Most decorative techniques can be applied to porcelain quite successfully but since it is such a pure material much porcelain is best left undecorated.

Soft clay can be impressed with biscuit wooden or plaster stamps. Fig. 28 shows a few of the many everyday objects that can be pressed into soft clay to create interesting textures and patterns. Pushed through a household sieve (see Fig. 29) soft clay makes 'hair' for sculptural work and can form decorative areas on pinch pots, round the rims or even inside the pots. Pieces left sticking out too far on a pot will get broken off easily. The sieved clay is joined on with slurry.

Leather hard clay can be pierced and carved with sharp tools. Since it is a smooth clay, porcelain cuts very well at this stage. Drill bits can be used to make small decorative holes. Use a sponge to smooth any rough edges. Engraving into leather hard clay is described in Chapter 4. Slips can be used for thin lines, thick bands and geometric shapes or random areas can be painted with coloured slips on to leather hard bodies. Interesting matt surfaces can be achieved by glaze firing such pieces unglazed. Alternatively, transparent or light glazes can be applied.

Porcelain can be engraved and cut into and inlaid with

coloured slips or with soft coloured porcelain clay. These can be made from the same body as the pot, with the addition of body stains or oxides. Using coloured clays made from the same body will decrease the risk of shrinkage differences between inlaid clay and pot. Chapter 7 describes how Audrey Blackman uses body stains to make coloured porcelain clays. By experimenting with varying amounts of stain, subtle effects can be achieved. All the leading pottery firms supply body stains and recommend the percentages to use in both their catalogues and with the products.

Fig. 28 Various textures can be made by pressing natural or man-made objects into the soft clay. *Photograph by C Paul Wilson*

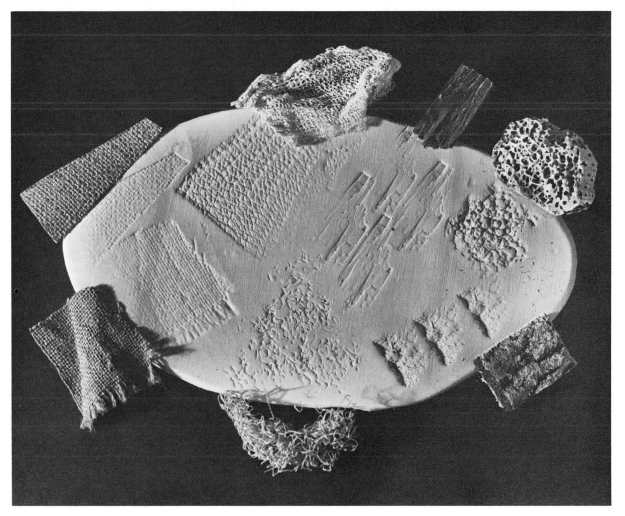

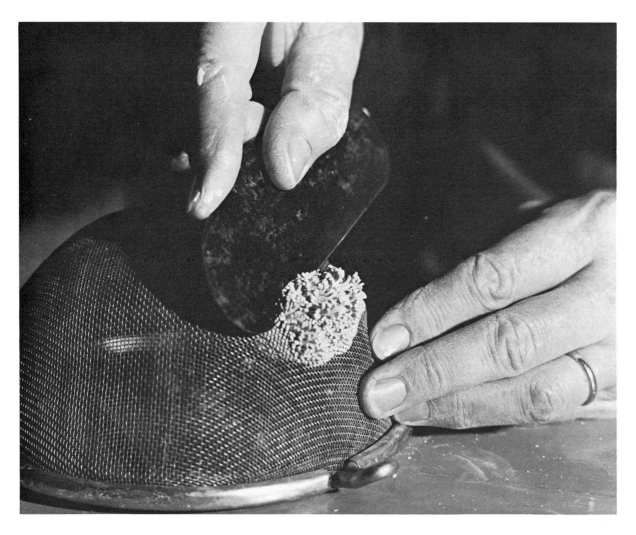

Fig. 29 Mary Rogers removing clay with a metal kidney after the clay has been pushed through a household sieve.
Photograph by Edward Piper

Using oxides:
Red iron oxide. 2—4 per cent for red/browns. Try less than 2 per cent as well.
Copper carbonate. 1—5 per cent for greens in oxidation and pinks and reds in reduction.
Cobalt. 0.5—2.5 per cent for light to dark blues.
Manganese carbonate will give an even brown colour.
Manganese dioxide (coarse) will give speckled effects.
2—10 per cent manganese is usual.

Colours will vary considerably depending on the firing atmosphere.

For inlaying, cut or score 1 to 3 mm ($\frac{1}{16}$ in. to $\frac{1}{8}$ in.) deep. The soft clay is inlaid and left to become leather hard and then any excess can be scraped away with a blade. This scraping also redefines the pattern or design. The main problem with inlaying into porcelain is the possibility of contaminating the white body with the coloured clays or slips. Stoneware clays can be inlaid into porcelain and vice versa, but if the shrinkage rates are very different, the inlaid clay may shrink away from the groove sides. Try inlaying on test pieces before committing the technique to pots. Also test inlaid pieces glazed and unglazed. One point to remember is that fired porcelain unglazed does get dirty from constant handling, but a good wash soon solves the problem.

Another exciting way of using coloured clays is described by Paulus Berensohn in his book *Finding One's Way with Clay* (see Bibliography, page 92). Some of the techniques can be tried out with coloured porcelain clays and white porcelain.

Drying

After decorating and finishing off leave the pieces to dry out naturally. Avoid fast drying from plastic to leather hard as this is when most shrinkage, which can cause warping or cracking, takes place. Even more important, avoid uneven drying for the same reasons. Dry porcelain is very fragile and needs to be handled with great care. Avoid constant handling and whenever possible leave a pot in one place to await firing.

General hints

Avoid rusty tools when working with porcelain. A good solution is to keep a separate tool box for the more common tools that you may use for various pottery jobs. Always check that polythene being used to wrap up porcelain is clean. Polythene bags are handy for wrapping up small pieces. A thin piece of foam is useful for resting thin pots down on their rim. Rolling porcelain out on wood may dry it out too quickly if it is going to be used for hand-building in the soft condition. Try damping the wood, and allow to dry for a while. The wood will not absorb moisture to such a degree after this.

4 Throwing, Turning and Joining Porcelain

Porcelain is an exciting but fairly difficult body to work with on the wheel. Compared with the more plastic clays it demands greater concentration and a more direct approach. For throwing it is important to get to know the material and this only comes with practice. It is difficult to say when one should start throwing with porcelain. There are certainly no rules. If you feel satisfied with your throwing experience, have a go. If porcelain proves too difficult to work with then there is not a lot of point in struggling. Far better to continue improving with a stoneware body and try porcelain again later. Many potters go for years without using porcelain. Then one day they have a go and find the change a fairly natural transition, although there may be a few initial problems to overcome. Use as plastic a porcelain body as possible for throwing.

Preparation

Before a throwing session thoroughly clean out the wheel, tools and working surfaces including the wedging bench. Also clean up boards and throwing bats in advance. If practical, devote some days to throwing with porcelain. This will not only build up a good rhythm of work but also eliminate endless cleaning up. Separate tools for porcelain only may prove useful. After use dry any metal tools to avoid rust which will contaminate the white clay.

Hand-kneading will put porcelain into a good condition for throwing. Wood is an ideal surface to knead on. If the clay is too soft, kneading it on a clean plaster bat will absorb some moisture and stiffen up the clay. Remember that drying porcelain on plaster tends to undo ageing and makes the body short. This can be avoided by leaving the clay to stiffen up naturally, by exposing it to the air. For throwing use fairly stiff clay, as soft clay will collapse easily on the wheel. David Leach uses stiff clay which is almost cracking as he kneads it.

Throwing

With porcelain it is important to know in advance the exact shape required and to throw in a direct and decisive way. Porcelain will not take being 'pushed around' like some stoneware bodies.

Fig. 30 Throwing a bowl. After centring and opening up, the walls are thinned out in a careful direct way.
Photograph by C Paul Wilson

Fig. 31 Fingers are used for final thinning and shaping.
Photograph by C Paul Wilson

Fig. 32 A reasonable amount of clay, which will be turned off, is left at this stage at the base to give support.
Photograph by C Paul Wilson

Structurally and visually a pot will be stronger if thrown fairly quickly. Porcelain is a fine smooth clay that can be thrown thinly but once the final shape is reached no more adjustments, which can often cause instant collapse, should be made. Since porcelain almost demands to be potted thin and in a precise way, it is easy to become so involved with this aspect that cold austere pots result. Hence the need to allow spontaneity to continue even when throwing with porcelain. Thickly thrown pots in porcelain often present a refreshing alternative to thin translucent pieces: while not obviously translucent they do retain a certain vigour and life.

Always approach a pot gently on the wheel, as any jerky action will cause it to go off centre. Most porcelain bodies are thirsty to throw with, so use enough water to stop the clay drying, catching and tearing. This is another good reason for fairly quick throwing as the amount of water being absorbed by the clay can cause it to soften and collapse. For the same reason, avoid leaving water in the bottom of the pot for too long while throwing. A creamy slurry is produced while throwing and some potters prefer to use this instead of water. It can, however, form a slight barrier in that it makes it difficult to sense the thickness of clay.

Shapes

Simple shapes work best in porcelain. Since it is not a very plastic clay newcomers should limit sizes to 15 cm (6 in.) wide and 20 cm (8 in.) high. A natural size limit is around 30 cm (12 in.) for thin translucent or semi-translucent pots. When making any shape remember that porcelain will sit or slump in the kiln far easier than other clays, particularly with large pots. Weak spots always seem to get worse quicker with porcelain than other clays (see Figs. 52 and 53). Pots with weak spots will almost certainly distort and slump in the kiln so they should be discarded at the throwing stage. Avoid excessive overhangs, particularly on plates and bowls.

Cylinders and bowls are good shapes to practise with. Cylinders are a useful indication of how thin the clay can be thrown. Cut some in half and examine the section. For small pots around 3 mm ($\frac{1}{8}$ in.) and less is a good thickness to aim for. Throwing different bowl shapes will indicate the limitations of

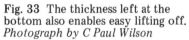

Fig. 33 The thickness left at the bottom also enables easy lifting off. *Photograph by C Paul Wilson*

Fig. 34 (*top right*) Direct form of Chinese bowl. Decorated in 'an hua' white slip under the glaze. Yung Lo, 1403—24. Ming monochrome ware. *Victoria and Albert Museum*

Fig. 35 Bowl by Marianne de Trey with wax resist and slip decoration. 8.5 cm wide, 3.5 cm high. *Photograph by Sue Barker*

the body. Bowls with a strong direct lift keep their shape well (see Fig. 34). They look strong. Very shallow flat or low bellied shapes will either sag during throwing or slump in the firing. Shallow dishes with a strong lift lend themselves well to incised-decoration.

Plates and saucers are often considered the most difficult shapes to make in porcelain. Give saucers an exaggerated upward curve so that they will keep their shape in the firing. Plates are best left until one has become very skilful as the risks of warping and cracking are high.

Lidded boxes require precision made with any clay and are a favourite with potters who use porcelain. For a really good lid fit use two pairs of calipers as shown in Figs. 37 and 38. One problem you may meet is that having thrown the base to the required size it is easy to open the lid out too far and almost impossible to bring it back. Only practice will overcome this problem. An interesting development of the lidded box is to throw the two halves really thick and then cut the sides into four, six or more facets when leather hard or softer. This can also be done on bowls and straight sided dishes. Fluting can be done on various leather hard shapes with a metal or bamboo fluting tool. The cut edges of cut sided or fluted pots cause the glaze to break which gives a pleasing effect especially with celadons.

Bigger thick-walled pots can be made in porcelain but they will not be translucent. Large pots can be made by throwing up so far, leaving the pot to dry a little and then developing with further throwing later. Care should be taken to allow the pot to dry evenly to avoid warping.

The technique of making large pots in two pieces is also possible with porcelain. Remember that with all large pots the distribution of weight in relation to the thickness of walls must be right. A thin place in the wall down at the bottom where it should be thick will give trouble. Aim to get the thickness of the two halves the same. A thinner bottom half may give way in the firing. In many cases it may be wiser to use a white stone-ware body for really large pots to avoid some of the problems. Porcelain usually works better on a small scale. Necks and feet can be thrown on by the usual coil and throw method. This technique should be carried out when the pot has stiffened up sufficiently to take the joining on of a fat coil by scoring and using slurry. The coil is then thrown up into a neck or foot

Fig. 36 (*overleaf left*) Throwing the bottom half of a lidded box. Forming the flange.
Photograph by C Paul Wilson

Figs. 37 and 38 (*overleaf right*) The lid is thrown and calipers are used to measure both the inside width and the outside.
Photograph by C Paul Wilson

51

Fig. 39 Turning the bottom half
of the lidded box.
Photography by C Paul Wilson

using as little water as possible.

Compared with other clays porcelain needs more support at the throwing stage. This means that a lot of thickness is left to be turned off when the pot is leather hard. Leave at least 1.25 cm ($\frac{1}{2}$ in.) thickness at the bottom of pots that will have a foot-ring turned. As pots get larger the thickness will have to be increased. If you have a lot of trouble with cracks in bases try leaving less thickness at the throwing stage. This will allow walls and base to dry more evenly. Flat-bottomed pots such as bottles and jars, which do not need turning or only require a quick skim at the turning stage, can be thrown to the same thickness as the walls.

Throwing on wheel bats

Whether to throw porcelain on bats or straight on the wheel-head is a matter of personal choice. Very large pots will need to be thrown on bats to avoid distortion. If fairly stiff clay is used for throwing many small shapes can be made on the wheel-head, cut, and lifted off successfully as long as the pot has not absorbed too much water. If a pot is lifted off the wheel in such a way that it distorts but goes round again, then it may well distort

Fig. 40 Incising the lid top with a
bamboo tool at the leather hard
stage.
Photograph by C Paul Wilson

Fig. 41 Incised decoration can be
filled in with colour. In the photograph on the left a mixture of
cobalt and manganese is inlaid
into the incised lines, when the clay
is leather hard. When the clay is dry
the excess colour is scraped away
with a razor blade leaving colour in
the incised lines only (*right*).
Photograph by C Paul Wilson

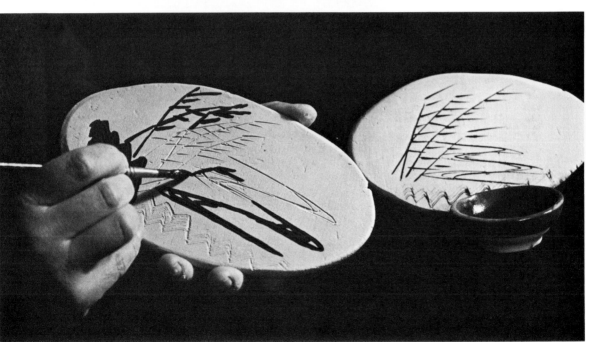

Fig. 42 David Leach fluting a teapot
with a bamboo tool.
Photograph by C Paul Wilson

Fig. 43 (*right*) David Leach throwing a teapot and forming the shape.

again in the firing. Porcelain appears to have a 'plastic' memory and can warp while drying or in the firing if it has been
misshapen during throwing. To reduce this risk of distortion
potters prefer to throw on bats. These can be plaster, wood or
asbestos. Pots cut with a twisted wire will lift off well. Porcelain
can distort easily as the wire passes through, particularly if the
walls are very thin. To avoid this try cutting through with the
wheel going round slower than usual. A thin single stranded wire
will disturb the pot very little. Pots should be removed from bats
as soon as they can be released, and placed on wooden boards to
enable base and walls to dry out evenly.

Ribs

Ribs can be very useful for throwing with porcelain since they
eliminate throwing rings. Again, their use is a matter of personal
choice. They can give a straight clean cut surface to a pot. You
may find it easier to feel the clay thickness without using a rib,
in which case throwing rings can be removed at the turning stage.
Ribs are useful for smoothing the insides of bowls, saucers and

plates. They also help to lift the clay, especially on larger pots. For narrow-necked pots a Japanese throwing stick (egote), or a small sponge on a stick, can be used like an interior rib while throwing.

Fig. 44 (*left*) Forming the galley.

Fig. 45 (*above*) Using the trimming stick to remove excess slurry and help form the shape.

Drying and turning

Remember that porcelain tends to dry out far quicker than other clays. Dry it out to leather hard for turning. If a pot is still a little flexible there is less risk of it cracking when being attached to the wheel-head or being taken off. Thin pots with thick bases will warp if not dried out evenly. Thin rims which dry out in advance of the rest of the pot can be damped down with a sponge or quickly dipped in water. The thicker bases sometimes need putting on a plaster bat or the pot can simply be turned upside down to allow them to dry out. Wide-based pots, such as shallow bowls, may bow if turned upside down so they are best left to dry the right way up.

Turning porcelain is an enjoyable technique; being a smooth body it responds well to sharp turning tools. There is a theory

Fig. 46 Throwing the spout.

Fig. 47 Final shaping of spout. The top is levelled off with a pin.

that turning porcelain reduces the possibility of S-cracks forming during drying or firing. S-cracks develop in the base because that part of the pot gets less compression than the walls during throwing. A turning tool run over the base can help to compress the clay. Turning the clay on the soft side of leather hard can also reduce the possibility of cracking, especially on lidded boxes. Cracks may also develop in bases because although you should try to dry pots as evenly as possible, it is inevitable that some bases will dry too slowly. Being such a fine smooth body, porcelain usually benefits from turning. Bowls, cups, saucers and dishes look good with foot-rings but thickly thrown lidded jars and dishes work equally well without feet. Lidded boxes can be turned in a precise way or in a freer, fresh, direct way.

Pots can be turned straight on the wheel-head, or in a chum or chuck or on a clay pad. The Chinese often turned their pots all the way down for really thin translucent walls. Some potters do this while others throw most of the pot to the final thickness and only turn the lower wall and foot. From a visual point of view it is best to remove throwing rings as they disturb the form from base through to rim. Very widely spaced throwing marks on the

Fig. 48 Cutting the spout with a sharp knife to fit teapot.
Last six photographs by Edward Piper

Figs. 49, 50 and 51 David Leach turning a foot-ring. A sharp turning tool is used and the pot is attached straight down on the wheel-head.
Photographs by Edward Piper

thicker more vigorous pots look fine.

It is very important to centre pots perfectly on the wheel to avoid uneven thicknesses which could cause warping. Sharp turning tools are essential for precise, crisp turning. However, a turning tool that is too sharp or blunt can cause juddering or chattering: use the heavy metal type for leather hard turning and a hoop tool for soft. A metal kidney can be used to skim over bases that are to be left flat. Alternatively, flat bases can be left as cut. If a pot has been stuck down on the wheel-head for turning and is difficult to release then a sharp tap on the side of the wheel-head should do the trick.

Some bentonite porcelains can soften while being turned, in rather the same way as wet sand reacts to being stood upon. Bodies containing up to 5 per cent bentonite should not give this problem.

Joining

The alternative to turning a foot-ring is to throw one on. A foot can be thrown separately and joined when leather hard to the

leather hard pot, or a coil can be added to the pot when it is
softer than leather hard, and thrown on the pot. After joining on
a leather hard foot-ring some turning may be necessary to form
an even flow between foot and pot.

Additions such as lugs, spouts and handles are liable to crack
in the later stages of drying. For this reason additions should be
as near the same hardness as the pot to which they are joined.
The usual methods of scoring and adding slurry or slip before
joining works well. Porcelain slurry does dry out quicker than
other clays. Excess slurry that oozes out can be bonded in when
it has dried to the plastic state. This forms good reinforcement.
Excess slurry can also be scraped away with a sharp knife or
blade. Once pieces have been added on, a pot should be dried
out as slowly as possible. Any addition that sticks out from the
pot will tend to dry out and shrink in advance of the pot. This
can cause cracking at the join. Joining at the leather hard stage
is usual but if you do get trouble with cracking try joining
pieces on the soft side to pots at the same stage. Little cracks in
porcelain are not disastrous and repair well. They can be
modelled and compressed in with a small blunt modelling tool.

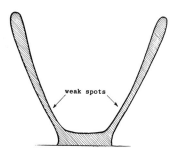

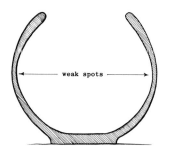

Figs. 52 and 53 Weakspots. Avoid
different thicknesses in the section
of a pot.

Larger cracks can be filled in with fairly hard clay. The sides of
the cracks may need to be dampened slightly so that the repair
does not dry out too quickly and crack again. Smooth repair
marks over with a damp natural sponge.

Holes in lugs can be made with a drill bit. Drill slowly and
carefully as the clay can tear at the leather hard stage. Use a damp
natural sponge to smooth the sharp edges. Most porcelain teapots
are made with lugs to take a cane handle, as a large pulled handle
can itself deform or pull the pot out of shape. Smaller handles on
teacups, mugs or jugs are possible but require much skill to
produce good results. There is always the likelihood that any-
thing joined to the side of a porcelain pot will pull it out of shape.
David Leach's very fine handled teacups are worth careful study.
He pulls the handles to the final size and dries them to the state
where they will bend without cracking. He then joins them to the
cups, scoring the joining area and using a little slurry, and bonds
the top join in with a small modelling tool. The bottom is joined
with a fingered fishtail end. When throwing, David Leach
deliberately leaves the handle attachment area slightly thicker.
This gives added strength and helps to stop the handle pulling
the pot out of round. It is very important to keep pots in the
right state for handling while the handles are being made. Keep
them wrapped in plastic if necessary. Porcelain can change colour
very quickly and become too hard for attachments to be made.

Pieces for joining on, such as lugs, can be made from slabs, or
thrown pots cut up. Rolled or cut slabs added to thrown pots
can set up a certain amount of pull and cause distortion. Thrown
additions are less likely to cause distortion as they will contain
the same kind of stress and tension as the thrown pot.

5 Porcelain Glazes

A porcelain glaze should be similar in composition to the body to ensure a good fit. For this reason feldspar, china clay and quartz are some of the main porcelain glaze ingredients as well as Cornish stone, nepheline syenite and whiting. Other useful materials are ash, dolomite, talc, ball clay, petalite and red iron oxide. Experience with stoneware glazes is extremely useful when developing glazes for porcelain, as many of the points relevant to stoneware glazes and materials are equally applicable to porcelain.

Feldspar
Feldspar is the most important ingredient in porcelain glazes and is the principal flux. It contains the glass modifiers and fluxes, soda and potash, and begins to melt at 1160—1180°C, forming a viscous glaze at cone 10. Feldspar also contributes alumina and silica to the glaze. The viscous nature of molten feldspar prevents glazes from running off the pot.

    Porcelain glaze recipes are usually very simple and high in silica. By adding a few of the above mentioned materials to feldspar good glazes can be developed. One of the classic porcelain recipes, Salvat's Modern Chinese Porcelain Glaze, proves the point.

Feldspar	39.6	Cone 8—10
Whiting	21.6	A smooth bright glaze that fits
China clay	9.7	well on porcelain bodies.
Quartz	29.1	

Fig. 54 Fluted bowl by David
Leach. Celadon glaze.
Photograph by Sue Barker

Fig. 55 (*opposite*) Jar painted in
underglaze red. Korean 17th—18th
century. Height 20 cm.
Victoria and Albert Museum

Cornish stone (Cornwall stone)
Used instead of feldspar it produces good results but has a
slightly higher melting point than feldspar. It also contains more
silica than feldspar and tests have shown that glazes containing
Cornish stone are less prone to crazing. They also tend to have a
smoother feel to them. For examples see the Recipe List below.

Nepheline syenite
Can be used as a substitute for some, or all of the feldspar, but it
does have a lower melting point. Nepheline can give unusual and
interesting results. Numbers 17 and 18 in the Recipe List are
particularly suitable for sculptural pieces.

Petalite
A flux that can be used as a substitute for some of the feldspar as
in Recipe 20. It contains lithia which has a low thermal expansion,
useful in preventing crazing.

Quartz or Flint
Provides the essential silica in porcelain glazes which, with its
low thermal expansion, lessens the tendency to crazing. Silica is
also the principal glass former.

Whiting
Introduces calcium into the glazes. Amounts of up to 25 per cent
can be used. An excess of whiting in a glaze will cause it to lose
its brightness.

Dolomite
Contains calcium and magnesium and is especially useful in
porcelain glazes as it gives a smooth surface. Up to 20 per cent can
be used.

Talc
Can be used to give a semi-matt effect to a glaze surface. It also
helps to decrease the thermal expansion of a glaze.

Many stoneware glazes fit well on porcelain bodies fired up to
around 1280—1300°C, provided they contain sufficient silica.
One way to develop porcelain glazes is by trying out all available
stoneware glazes and making adjustments if necessary. There may

Fig. 56 Small teapot by Bernard Leach. Pale celadon glaze.
Photograph by Peter Kinnear

Fig. 57 Bowl by Emmanuel Cooper. Pale green speckled and crackled nepheline syenite glaze with a small percentage of copper.

be some surprises. It is always good to find a stoneware glaze that works well on porcelain. Celadons are a good example of this. After first tests some glazes can be eliminated if fired colour or surface texture is not satisfactory.

Adjustments can be made by taking the recipe back to its formula using the Seger Formula*. For example the silica content may need increasing or the potash/soda content decreasing. After adjustments, convert back to a recipe for further trials. The empirical, trial and error, method of making adjustments to a recipe can also be used.

The formulae of Seger Cones are useful for evolving recipes for certain temperatures. The cones melt to a glaze three or four cones higher than their bending temperature. For example, one could calculate the cone 7 formula ($RO \quad Al_2O_3 \, 0.7 \quad SiO_2 \, 7.0$) recipe and test fire it at cone 10.

Faults

Crazing

Although crazing is a fault it is only really necessary to adjust a crazed glaze if the crazing is excessive. Many potters make use of crazing glazes for various reasons. The crackle can be stained with red iron oxide, manganese, or tea, for a decorative effect. Fine crazing can hardly be detected by the eye and indeed some of the finest glazes on porcelain are crazed.

A glaze should hold a pot in a state of slight compression, giving it strength. During cooling the body and glaze contract. If the glaze shrinks more than the body, then it will craze. This can be cured by increasing the silica content of the glaze. This will decrease its thermal expansion and give a better fit. If a lot of

Fig. 58 Bowl covered with a pale celadon-green crackled glaze. Chinese Sung Dynasty. Height 9.5 cm, diameter 11.8 cm. *Victoria and Albert Museum*

*Seger Formula. A method of representing the composition of a glaze that assists comparison, assessment and adjustment. The chemical composition is recalculated to molecular fractions and the constituent oxides are then arranged in three groups Alkaline (RO) Intermediate (R_2O_3) and Acid (RO_2). The Alkaline group adds up to unity.
Example: *Seger Cone 7 to 9 porcelain glaze*

RO Group	R_2O_3 Group	RO_2 Group
.3K_2O	.4Al_2O_3	4SiO_2
.7CaO		
(unity)		

trouble is experienced with glazes crazing then it often makes more sense to adjust the silica content of the body (see page 18).

The thickness of a glaze on porcelain is important and some glazes will only craze where applied too thickly. Glazes on ball clay porcelains are less prone to crazing.

N.B. Pots used for food ideally should not be crazed.

Shivering and shattering
These faults should not be experienced if standard porcelain bodies and glazes are used. The shivering of a glaze and shattering of a body are caused by an excess of free quartz and cristobalite and cured by decreasing the silica content in glaze and body respectively.

Crawling
Apart from all the usual reasons for crawling, glazes on porcelain do tend to crawl or peel on rims. This happens especially on the thin rims of bowls where a double thickness of glaze builds up if the pouring and dripping method is used. To avoid this, after glazing the inside of a bowl quickly scrape off the glaze on the rim before dipping the outside. This will leave only a thin single layer of glaze on the rim. Some potters prefer to scrape the rim glaze thin after inside and outside have been glazed.

Pin-holing
Many stoneware glazes work best when applied fairly thinly to porcelain. If used too thick pin-holing may occur. Overfiring can also cause a glaze to pin-hole.

Application

Glazes can be applied to porcelain at the raw or biscuit stage and, in general, glazing porcelain is little different from glazing stoneware. The temperature at which pots are biscuit fired will, of course, determine porosity (see page 77). Porcelain that has had rather a low biscuit ($900-950°C$) will be very porous and thin glazes should be used, to avoid thick layers being built up.

Thin walled pots will not absorb a lot of glaze and can become saturated or may even stay wet for quite a while. This is bad as it can cause a glaze to crawl in the early stages of the firing, due to the large amount of moisture in the biscuit pot and the glaze being driven off too quickly. Therefore for thin walled pots it

Fig. 59 Box, thrown and turned by Emmanuel Cooper. Vanadium glaze with brown and pink spots. 6.25 cm tall.

may be necessary to use thick glazes or to dry such pots artificially after glazing.

Watch out for dusty surfaces on biscuit or raw pots especially on more sculptural work that has been scraped when the clay was dry. Give such pieces a good dust with a soft brush before glazing. Remember that thin walled porcelain can be very fragile, so take care when handling during the glazing process. It is essential to coat the unglazed surfaces of lidded pots with alumina mixed with china clay and water, or alumina hydrate or any other form of wash to prevent lids sticking. If wax is used to prevent glaze adhering where lid and pot touch, then the alumina wash will have to be applied before the wax. Lids fired *in situ* will help to keep the pot in shape. A lidded box can be fired with small rolls of china clay between lid and box. If this method is used the rolls should be of equal thickness and after placing on the box, the lid lightly squashed on. This ensures a good fit, and prevents the rolls being knocked out during packing of the kiln. After firing the lid separates easily and the rolls knock off without any damage to the pot.

Fig. 60 Chinese bowl with light bluish-green glaze. Ying Ch'ing type. 12—13th century. Diameter 19.5 cm, height 8 cm.
Victoria and Albert Museum

Fig. 61 Chinese dish, Sung Dynasty. Savier porcelain, 'Northern celadon' ware with incised decoration.
Victoria and Albert Museum

Fig. 62 Group of lidded pots with trailed glaze by Janet Leach.
Photograph by Peter Kinnear

Pouring and dipping

The pouring and dipping method of glazing is quite straight-forward for porcelain, but see section on 'Crawling' on page 68. In most cases glazes should be used thinner than for stoneware or the pouring and dipping has to be done very quickly. It is always worth waxing areas on pots, like lidded boxes, where two halves will be fired together but with the dipping process it is not necessary to wax bases.

Spraying

Spraying is useful for sculptural pieces that are difficult to dip, and also for raw glazing where it is difficult to handle a pot without breaking bits off it. Remember that it is easy to build up thick or uneven layers of glaze with the spraying process. Thick glazes on porcelain tend to give a coated effect. A glaze looks well when there is not a marked difference between pot and glaze. Spraying is also useful in avoiding the double layer of glaze building up on rims as it does with dipping.

Once-fired glazing

Porcelain can be successfully glazed at the raw or green stage and it is well worth trying. Written information on once-firing is available and the general rules can be applied to porcelain. Lucie Rie raw glazes her porcelain by brushing on the glaze. Once-firing porcelain eliminates the need to pack pieces twice in the kiln and therefore reduces the risk of breakage, but, equally, there are hazards in applying liquid glaze to leather hard or dry pots.

Ideally, once-fired glazes should contain at least 25 per cent clay. China clay should not be used as it is not a plastic clay. Ball clay can be substituted for china clay. Some potters glaze raw ware at the leather hard stage as glazes applied to dry pots can blister and lift off as they dry. However, by heating dry pots before glazing, the glaze and pot dry quickly after glazing and no blisters will form. An interval between glazing the inside and outside will allow the pot to dry, and dry pots can be glazed in this way without heating.

Glaze recipes

Glaze recipes are abundant these days and in addition to this list, the books mentioned in the Bibliography on page 92 will contain more recipes. *Ceramic Review* and *Pottery Quarterly* also often contain useful recipes. It is important to experiment with glazes on porcelain and to be prepared to make adjustments if necessary.

1	*WHITE*	1280°C
	Cornish stone	80
	Whiting	20
	China clay	20

Very good glaze on porcelain. Fits well. Smooth feel.

2	*CELADON*	1280°C
	Cornish stone	80
	Whiting	20
	China clay	20
	Red iron oxide	2

Works best in reduction firing. Good fit on porcelain although it crazes slightly on non-ballclay porcelains. Use fairly thickly.

3	*SATIN WHITE*	1280°C
	Cornish stone	60
	Dolomite	20
	China clay	20

Very good fit on porcelain. Sometimes gives a mottled effect. Do not use too thickly.

4	*TEMMOKU*	1280°C
	Cornish stone	74
	Whiting	11
	Quartz	15
	Red iron oxide	10

5	*ASH GLAZE*	Cone 8—10
	Potash feldspar	70 or 80
	Ash	30 or 20

One of the classic ash glaze recipes. It does craze but some very subtle effects can be achieved, especially in a reduction firing, using an iron-bearing ash.

6	*WHITE/YELLOW MOTTLED GLAZE*	1280°C
	Cornish stone	30
	China clay	20
	Whiting	20
	Talc	10

Good fit. Best in reduction firing. A 'coating' type glaze.

7	*Audrey Blackman GLAZE — SHINY*	1290°C (Electric kiln)
	Cornish stone	20
	China clay	30
	Whiting	23
	Quartz	27

8	*Audrey Blackman GLAZE — MATT*	1280°C (Electric kiln)
	Feldspar	56
	China clay	24
	Dolomite	24
	Whiting	2

9	*Vera Acheson GLAZE*	1280°C
	Feldspar	30
	Whiting	16
	Talc	12
	China clay	24
	T W V D ballclay	6
	Quartz	12

Works best in reduction, and on Podmore's David Leach body.

10	*Daniel Rhodes CORNISH STONE GLAZE*	Cones 9—10
	Cornish stone	85
	Whiting	15

This glaze in analysis is similar to a Chinese porcelain glaze. Used thickly, it gives an opaque smooth surface and crazes over most clays.

11	*Daniel Rhodes CORNISH STONE GLAZE*	Cones 9—10
	China clay	15.7
	Quartz	26.7
	Dolomite	4.5
	Zinc oxide	1.5
	Whiting	10.9
	Cornish stone	40.6

A smooth bright glaze. By rounding the above figures off, Marianne de Trey finds the following works well on porcelain.

12		Cones 9—10
	China clay	16
	Quartz	27
	Dolomite	4
	Zinc oxide	1.5
	Whiting	11
	Cornish stone	41

13	*Marianne de Trey ASH GLAZE*	Reduction
	Ash	33
	Feldspar	33
	Quartz	33
	Bentonite	3

14 *Robert Fournier STANDARD STONEWARE WHITE*

	1275°C
Feldspar	40
Nepheline syenite	20
Whiting	15
China clay	10
Talc	10
Flint	5

This stoneware glaze works quite well on porcelain. It may craze and it does have a tendency to slip or peel on rims, so glaze should be scraped thin. At 1265°C it often has a slight orange peel texture like saltglaze.

15 *John Reeve SMOOTH BRIGHT GLAZE*

	Cones 8—10
Feldspar	27
Ballclay	14
China clay	7
Whiting	20.5
Quartz	31.5

16 *David Leach CONE 8 GLAZE*

Feldspar or Cornish stone	25
China clay	25
Whiting	25
Quartz	25

Good bright glaze. Smooth feel. For a Ying Ching type glaze add $\frac{1}{2}$ per cent iron oxide. For a celadon add 2 per cent iron oxide. N.B. There will be a tendency to craze if fired high, especially if feldspar is used instead of Cornish stone. Cone 8 to 9 is about right for the celadon.

17 *NEPHELINE SYENITE GLAZE*

	1280°C
Nepheline syenite	64
Whiting	8
China clay	8
Talc	8

Fits well on porcelain. Matt white/blue in reduction firing. Use thinly.

18　*Peter Simpson NEPHELINE SYENITE GLAZE*
1200—1220°C (Cone 6)

Nepheline syenite	74
Whiting	13
China clay	7
Quartz	8
Bone ash	1

Bone ash introduces an opalescence and a slight blueness to the glaze.

19　*Daniel Rhodes SMOOTH CLEAR GLAZE*　　Cone 10—12

Oxford spar (potash feldspar)	50.4
China clay	3.7
Quartz	24.9
Dolomite	2.6
Zinc oxide	1.1
Whiting	17.2

Rhodes recommends that this glaze should be used thinly.

20　*Petalite glaze from 'Illustrated Dictionary of Practical Pottery'*

Feldspar	12
Dolomite	12
Quartz	22
China clay	14
Ballclay	9
Petalite	28
Bentonite	3

A glaze that works well on the David Leach body.

6 Kiln Packing and Firing

Unless it is once-fired, porcelain goes through the normal biscuit and then glaze firing process.

Biscuit

The temperature at which porcelain is biscuit fired is not critical, although it does determine the porosity of biscuit ware for glazing. As mentioned in Chapter 5, low fired biscuit (around 900—950°C) can be very porous and fragile. It is therefore preferable to fire 950—1000°C. If small amounts of porcelain are being biscuit fired along with stoneware it will be practical to fire at the normal biscuit temperature. If this happens to be rather low then glazes may have to be thinned accordingly. Otherwise batches of porcelain can be fired at higher temperatures.

Even at biscuit temperatures, clay has what is known as pyroplasticity. Pots can deform if packed in such a way that there is uneven pressure. For example, avoid packing heavy pots on top of thin walled pots. Slabbed pots placed on top of round pots may have unsupported areas and will slump down. In general the normal methods of packing raw pots can be used: rim to rim, base to base. The thin rims of bowls and delicate handles should not be placed too near the elements in an electric kiln, or near direct flames, but this is more important in the glaze firing.

Glaze firing

Packing glazed biscuit pots in the kiln requires care both in handling and method. During the firing, porcelain, like other

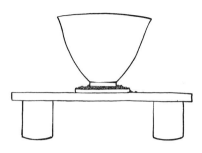

Fig. 63 There are two methods of placing pots in the kiln. Firstly, silica sand or alumina batwash, or alumina hydrate is spread on a disc and the pot is placed on top.

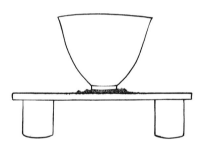

Fig. 64 The second method is to spread the silica sand or alumina hydrate straight on to the kiln shelf for the pot to sit on.

clays, expands slightly up to around 750°C and for this reason a space of at least 3 mm ($\frac{1}{8}$ in.) should be allowed between pots.

Once the clay starts to vitrify it also starts to shrink. This shrinkage is considerable with porcelain and will cause distortion if a pot is not allowed to move as it shrinks. Porcelain fired directly on shelves that are not coated with batwash or setting material will stick to the shelf as the clay vitrifies. As the clay shrinks it is unable to contract evenly and this results in the distortion of the shape of the pot and pieces of the pot will be left behind on the kiln shelf when unpacking. There are various ways of avoiding distortion and sticking down. Porcelain should always be placed on some kind of setting material. Pots can be fired on discs made from the same body as the pots. These discs should be batwashed all over and used only once. This method allows the pot and disc to move and shrink together at the same rate. As an extra precaution, the base of the pot could be brushed with a small amount of batwash. Alternatively, some potters use the refractory discs obtainable from kiln furniture suppliers. These too should be thoroughly batwashed and can be used again and again until they warp or break. (Buy discs at least 3 mm ($\frac{1}{8}$ in.) thick.) As shown in Fig. 63, these discs can be especially useful when kiln shelves are warped. Porcelain standing on warped shelves will distort as the clay softens during vitrification. When firing porcelain that is not exceptionally thin, a layer of silica sand on the flat shelf allows pots to move without distortion. In her saltglaze kiln, Mary Rich places her porcelain on a 3 mm ($\frac{1}{8}$ in.) layer of alumina hydrate in powder form. One of the most interesting ways the Chinese fired their porcelain tea-cups was to leave the rims unglazed and fire them on the rims to prevent distortion. After firing the rims were polished or rimmed with a metal band.

As clay vitrifies and softens to a semi-molten state, pots may slump or even collapse if the top half of the pot is heavier than the bottom. This problem is discussed on page 51. Pots with thin rims or handles placed directly next to elements or intense flames may also warp and distort. Some potters prefer to protect their porcelain pots by surrounding them with stoneware. Handles, lugs and other additions will tend to pull a pot out of shape, and for this reason handles especially should be as small and light as possible. Yet another reason for distortion

78

is the plastic memory of clay which is believed to be extreme in porcelain. If a pot has been unevenly dried or warped, then rounded again while soft, it may warp or distort again during the firing.

Other faults
Many faults that reveal themselves in the biscuit or glaze firing can be traced back to body composition, the making or glazing process. Making faults are discussed on pages 28 and 29. Crazing, shivering, shattering, crawling and pin-holing are all discussed in page 68.

Overfiring of a body will result in bloating or deformation and at worst collapse. Glazes will pool and run off the pot. Another reason for slumping or deformation is too much feldspar in the body. This may also cause the body to have a rather glassy look. A sugary texture will indicate that there is too much silica in the body.

There is no one temperature at which porcelain should be fired. Most craft potters fire porcelain between 1250—1300°C. Some fire higher. The Chinese and Japanese probably fired no higher than 1300°C, though in European industry it was necessary to fire between 1300—1450°C to achieve the required porcelain qualities with the material they were using. As already mentioned, many potters fire porcelain with stoneware and in those cases the stoneware firing temperature usually predetermines the firing temperature for porcelain. If a kiln fires rather unevenly, finding the place where porcelain fires best will be a matter of trial and error. Some flame kilns have cold and hot spots and the best results are sometimes achieved by firing porcelain in the cold spots.

The length of firing cycle is important and here some stoneware firing cycles may prove too short for porcelain. The more undissolved silica left in a body the less translucent it will be. For this reason porcelain bodies benefit from a fairly long soak towards the end of the firing (see Chapter 2). For example, if firing in an electric or flame kiln to cone 9, a soak from cone 8 onwards should give good results. Experiment with the length of soaking time and observe the results. John Reeve in his *Pottery Quarterly* article (see Bibliography, page 92) mentions an extremely long soak above cone 8 when firing to cone 10, which produced good qualities. In our oil fired kiln we fire to 1280°C over $14\frac{1}{2}$ hours, soaking cone 9 down over the last hour and then soaking for around half an hour at the top temperature.

Reduction and oxidation

Kiln atmosphere will affect the colour and sometimes the texture of body and glaze. A reducing atmosphere will give a bluish-white tinge to a porcelain body. This is due to the small amount of ferric iron present in a porcelain body which is changed to ferrous iron in the reducing atmosphere. Ferrous iron produces the blueness which makes a body seem whiter than it really is. The purity of materials used in a body will affect fired colour. If the bentonite or ballclay used is contaminated with iron then speckling will result if the iron is reduced. A grey white could be due to the use of an inferior china clay, or 'dirty' bentonite. No materials are completely free from impurities and most contain small amounts of iron oxide.

An oxidizing atmosphere will tend to give a warm yellow white to the body unless a cobalt bleaching stain is used.

Body texture can be affected by the type of firing used. If the rate of firing is too fast or there is insufficient ventilation for escaping gases, small bubbles or bloating may result on the body surface. Bloating is more likely to be the result of over-firing. It is worth noting that Lucie Rie, Mary Rogers, Peter Simpson and many other potters achieve excellent results with porcelain in electric kilns. Many of the superb Chinese porcelains such as the Ting wares were also fired in an oxidizing atmosphere.

The reduction firing too has its advantages. Celadons, copper reds and Ying Ching type glazes are the obvious examples. If reduction is started too early, before 800°C, the body or glaze may be stained grey by carbon. On porcelain this is very undesirable. There are many different reduction cycles. In our kiln we achieve good results with porcelain by starting reduction at 1000°C and continue until the end of the firing at 1280°C. Some potters oxidize for short periods in between reduction and some finish up with half an hour of oxidation at the end. Celadons are said to benefit from a fairly heavy reduction at the end of the firing.

7 Two Potters who use Porcelain

Audrey Blackman

Audrey Blackman trained as a sculptor and started making rolled pottery figures in 1948. Her figures catch life as it goes past. Events or split second happenings that attract Audrey Blackman's eye are recorded as a matchstick drawing or just in her mind. She has developed a photographic memory and finds that detailed drawings would only take away from the picture in her mind.

One interesting example of her work is 'Into the Wind' (Fig. 65), two young people on a cliff top with a blustery wind tossing their hair and billowing the girl's skirt. It is patterned by impressions which I shall describe later. Placed in sunlight it is beautifully translucent. This group has been glazed with a transparent glaze, then Audrey Blackman has added touches of onglaze colour. The whole effect is one of great liveliness.

Audrey Blackman's methods of making rolled pottery figures have evolved naturally over the years as have the types of clay she uses. The figures were first made in earthenware with underglaze decoration in clear colours, then in unglazed stoneware and, since 1971, in porcelain. Having enjoyed the matt surface and soft colours of stoneware, Audrey Blackman longed to get a real white effect. She uses the David Leach body from Podmores which stands up well during making, folds easily without cracking, and rolls out well if used in the right consistency.

A further development has been to use coloured porcelain clays. These are made up by adding different percentages of coloured stains to the white powdered porcelain clay. The mix is then sprinkled into water, dried out to a plastic state and then stored in polythene or aluminium tins.

Fig. 65 'Into the Wind' by Audrey Blackman.
Photograph by Thomas Photos, Oxford

81

Some examples;

Green	5 per cent of Blythe's Green stain
Lemon/Yellow	10 per cent of Blythe's Yellow stain
Orange	10 per cent of Blythe's Orange stain
Pink	5 per cent of Blythe's Pink stain

e.g. 50 g of yellow stain to 500 g of powdered porcelain. The coloured clays should be used sparingly since over-use gives a rather 'trite' effect. Various tones can be achieved by varying the percentages and different colours produced by mixing colours before adding to the porcelain powder. All of the leading pottery suppliers stock these body stains.

The coloured clays are used for various effects. For marbling: small rolls of two or three different coloured clays are rolled together into a single roll between the hands. The more rolling done at this stage the more marbled the effect will be. For a striped effect, only a small amount of rolling is necessary. The consistency of the clays must be just right; if sticky soft they will cling together and if too dry they will break up and crack when rolling out. If one colour is wetter than another it will spread further, overpower the other and the mass will become a single colour.

After hand-rolling the roll is laid down on to a flat surface and rolled out to a thin slab or sheet with a rolling pin. A sharp scalpel is used to cut the slab to size and to remove excess pieces on a figure as it is being built up. The woman's skirt in 'Women's Lib' (Fig. 67) was made in this way with four different coloured clays.

Coloured pieces of clay are also laid on the white clay and rolled in to give various effects, like the spots on the child's dress which are inlaid pink clay. All Audrey Blackman's figures are made with soft clay, carefully building up rolls and thin sheets. The loose folds in the clothing and the quality of movement in the figures could not be achieved with a stiff clay.

Working on a figure is a continuous process and although it may take between fifteen to fifty hours to finish one, it is maintained at the same consistency as far as possible. After work the piece is sprayed with water from a mouthspray, damp sponges are assembled round it, not touching the clay, and a polythene bag dropped over. The piece is also sprayed at the beginning of a working session. This damping down depends

on how dry the piece has become and the humidity of the atmosphere.

Slabs and folded pieces of clay are joined together with a thin slurry (slip) applied with a brush. Patterns are impressed on to the soft clay with biscuit fired stamps and tools, as on the lady's skirt in 'Into the Wind' (Fig. 65). Sheets of clay are variously impressed to achieve different effects. Strips of rubber matting, for example, may be pressed down on them to make corduroy, or net curtain material may be used to texture a jersey.

Arms, legs, and the torso are built up with rolls, while the 'drapery' is built up from thin sheets of clay, in such a way as to suggest muscle. A pair of legs is made from one roll of clay tapered down each end for the ankles, and the feet are pushed out. The modelling of limbs is important, since they are an obvious indication of age and, often, character. Faces are left blank and, surprisingly, express as much that way as if they had features.

Care is always taken not to trap any air in a figure which is being built up. Holes are made underneath slabbed steps or other built up bases to allow air to escape during firing. Thick sections

Fig. 66 'The Rocking Horse Winner' by Audrey Blackman

Fig. 67 'Women's Lib', bisque porcelain, by Audrey Blackman.

are scooped with a fine wire looped tool.

Clay is always wedged before use and as it is rolled out a careful watch is kept for air bubbles, which are pricked out if they appear. Although such small air bubbles would not cause any structural damage to a figure, slight bumps on the surface could impair the form.

As a figure is built up, wooden props are used for parts that need supporting. These are replaced by clay props (made at the same time and of the same porcelain clay) once the piece is nearly leather hard. The clay props are left in place for firing and are placed at such an angle that they touch the kiln bat and are removed afterwards. This is sometimes impossible under legs where there would have to be too sharp an angle to reach the kiln shelf. This is overcome by putting a hole in the base during making. The prop can touch the kiln bat through the hole and be removed after firing.

All figures are biscuit fired in an electric kiln to 955°C which gives them enough strength for handling. A thin dolomite glaze is sprayed on with a mouthspray, giving a new dimension to the finished figure. Some figures are left unglazed, and this works particularly well when coloured clays have been used, giving an all over matt effect. Audrey Blackman feels that often the shadows are all the more telling on the unglazed pieces and that the modelling shows up much more.

The white figures are glazed with a transparent shiny glaze and fired to 1280°C. Figures with coloured clays are glazed with a dolomite glaze and fired to 1260°C. Experiments may be made by firing unglazed figures through from raw to glaze temperatures in one firing.

Rolled pottery figures are an excellent way of working things out in the round — a kind of three-dimensional drawing. As a teaching technique they are ideal, but individual potters naturally develop their own methods of making. Working on a larger or smaller scale, in more detail or less, and by using different tools, the modeller is free to experiment.

Colin Pearson

Colin Pearson started to use porcelain just prior to an exhibition
at the Crafts Centre in London in 1971. He had never used it
before, feeling that his temperament was best suited to stoneware.
He had begun to find, however, that the results he required of
the winged forms he was making in stoneware were getting lost
in the glazes. The pots looked marvellous before glazing and firing
and he realized that they needed to be made in one colour only.
It seemed logical to try the forms out in white smooth porcelain
and a black, rough, highly grogged stoneware body. Both clays
worked well. The porcelain 'gave' a purity of form and, with just
a thin glaze, allowed everything achieved at the making stage to
be revealed after firing. At first all the pots were glazed white
with perhaps the occasional accidental flash of copper. Colour
was used on some pots and then the more sensuous glazes, such
as celadons, while still retaining the form of the object. A further
progression was making bowls with attachments, still in a non-
functional sense.

The winged forms combine thrown cylinders or bowls with
hand-made attachments. As Colin Pearson also makes functional
ware in stoneware it is necessary to clean everything up and spend
a few days or more using porcelain. He starts with a throwing ses-
ion which does not last very long compared with the total time
spent on the pieces. Although he has no fixed ideas of how the shapes
will turn out he finds that he has to start with a clearer conception
of the finished pot when working with porcelain than he does
with stoneware. The cylinders are thrown up so far with the
fingers and then ribs are used. Finger throwing does not suit this
type of work at all since the ridges detract from the form and
take over the surface. Ribs and knives of different shapes and
sizes are used, sometimes sharp, sometimes blunt. A short sharp
rib is used for a torn look, but porcelain is more difficult to tear
than stoneware. Colin Pearson likes using ribs to get the strength,
sharp angles and torn effects that give his throwing such power.
It is also possible to get a thinner section without having to wet
the body so much and thereby retaining the physical strength
of the piece. The rims of the cylinders are also treated with the
same direct approach. The ribs are used to give cut, sharp or
bevelled rims.

Colin Pearson throws porcelain fairly slowly and tries to let
unevenness and warping occur. He often prefers 'accidents' but

Fig. 68 Winged form by Colin
Pearson, 1971, height 30 cm.
Photograph: Pottery Quarterly

finds that spontaneity in the making may get out of hand in
the firing.

Having built up a collection of cylinders he wraps them in
plastic bags while the wings and other attachments are made.
These are made in a fairly random way. A couple of days may be
spent making all sorts of wings, building up a kind of library from
which selection can be made. Quite a lot get left over. The wings
are made by very clay-like processes. They are not built up in a
conceptual manner in the way many hand-builders work. Methods
are used which produce spontaneous, 'accidental' results. They
are all made by fairly rapid processes that are in keeping with the
type of throwing. A block of clay is used for making the wings.
Thin slices are cut from the block that has been plunged with
sticks, or gouged out or pierced. Different ways of dragging the
wire through are used. Oscillating the wire up and down, dragging
through a thick wire that has got kinks in it, changing directions —
all give different results. Some wings are combed, others carved
or modelled.

Wings and other attachments are joined to the basic cylinder
shape at the leather hard stage by the usual method of scoring
the surfaces, adding slurry and pushing together. The assembly
of a piece involves selecting and discarding attachments until
the right effect is achieved.

Colin Pearson often uses an overhead or side spotlight while
throwing, turning and assembling. When working on a tall
vertical pot he uses a light directly overhead so that what is
happening in terms of light and shape can be clearly seen. It is
also useful for seeing inside tall cylinders. For bowls and flatter
pieces a side spot is used for the same reasons and it enables a
clear view of the profile.

Bowls are thrown up to 15 cm or 17.5 cm (6 in. or 7 in.) wide
as thinly as possible. They are usually turned all the way down
as they need to be exceedingly thin. They are placed on biscuit
fired chucks (hollow cylinders with rounded tops) for turning,
never with rims straight on the wheel-head.

Although he has raw glazed porcelain Colin Pearson finds it
is worth biscuit firing to around 900—1000°C to give pieces
enough strength for handling during glazing. The winged forms
particularly need this strength, as during dipping into the glaze
bucket a sharp twist back and forward is given to force the
glaze into all the holes in the wings. If this were done on raw

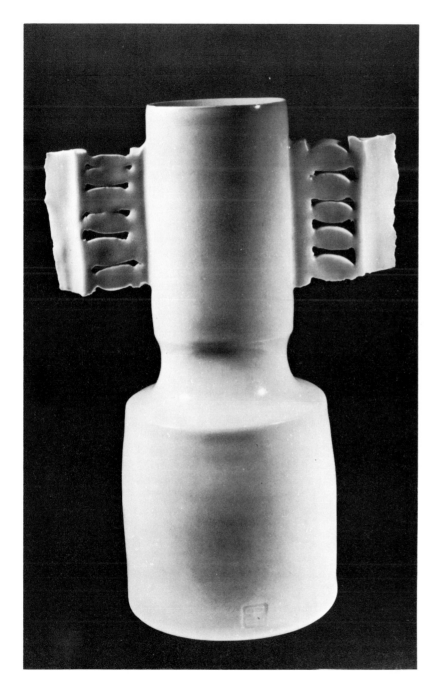

Fig. 69 Winged form by Colin Pearson.
Victoria and Albert Museum

pieces there would be a danger of wings falling off. When pieces are raw glazed they are sprayed and heated at the same time, but there is always the danger of raising a slight blister.

Normally the pieces are sprayed or dipped after biscuit firing. Spraying is time consuming and on intricate pieces it is hard to assess thickness. Unless a piece is very large most of the work is dipped. Thin-sectioned attachments are often heated with a gas torch before glazing so that they will take up the same thickness of glaze as the main structure. Colin finds it is worth re-glazing a piece he is not satisfied with and firing again.

Some glazes he uses particularly because they do craze and others because they do not. With his Ying Ching glaze he increased the alumina and silica to an extreme level and by doing a line blend picked out the first test that did not craze. The fluxes are kept balanced and the ratio of alumina and silica the same.

The porcelain is reduction fired together with stoneware in a gas kiln to cones 9—10. Reduction takes place from 930—950°C until the end of the firing. The normal precaution of placing the porcelain on setting rings is taken to keep the feet in shape. Other ware is used to protect the porcelain from the immediate heat.

For Colin Pearson, clay has its own way of behaving, its own logic, and it is his deep understanding of the clay that makes it possible for him to achieve the direct, strong, yet quiet qualities that are well worth studying in his porcelain forms.

Appendix 1 Suppliers' List

UK Suppliers

Porcelain clay bodies, raw materials for bodies, glazes and general pottery supplies

Podmore and Son Ltd, Shelton, Stoke, Staffs. ST1 4PQ.
  Tel. 0782-24571

Harrison Mayer Ltd, Meir, Stoke, Staffs. ST3 7PX. Tel. 0782-
  31611

The Fulham Pottery Ltd, 210 New King's Road, London
  SW6 4NY. Tel. 01-736-1188

Potclays Ltd, Brickkiln Lane, Etruria, Stoke, Staffs. ST4 7BP.
  Tel. 0782-29816

Wengers Ltd, Etruria, Stoke, Staffs. ST4 7BQ. Tel. 0782-
  25126

Raw materials

Degg Industrial Minerals Ltd, Phoenix Works, Webberley Lane,
  off Lightwood Road, Longton, Stoke, Staffs. ST3 1RJ.
  Tel. 0782-31077/8

The products of English China Clays Ltd, St. Austell, Cornwall,
PL25 4DJ are supplied to small users through appointed
distributors and clay blenders, and not direct to individual
potters.

Small lot distributors are:

Anchor Chemical Co. Ltd, Clayton, Manchester M11 4SR

Fordamin (Sales) Co. Ltd, Free Wharf, Brighton Road,
  Shoreham-by-Sea, Sussex

Somerville Agencies Ltd, Meadowside, Renfrew

Whitfield & Son Ltd, 23 Albert Street, Newcastle-under-Lyme, Staffs. ST5 1JP

N.B.

English China Clays Ltd. and Watts Blake Bearne & Co Ltd. will readily supply data sheets and general information on their products.

The Fulham Pottery Ltd. supply English China Clay's Standard Porcelain China Clay.

Ball clays and china clays
Watts Blake Bearne & Co Ltd, Park House, Courtenay Park, Newton Abbot, Devon TQ12 4PS. Tel. 0626-2345

Stains, colours for decoration and pottery supplies
Deancraft Ceramic Supplies, The Craft Division of Blythe Colours Ltd, 15/21 Westmill Street, Hanley, Stoke, Staffs. ST1 3EN. Tel. 0782-267226

Bentonite
Colin Stewart Minerals Ltd. Wharton Lodge Mills, Nat Lane, Winsford, Cheshire CW7 3BU. Tel. 06065-2291/2/3

Steetley Minerals Ltd, Woburn Road, Woburn Sands, Milton Keynes MK17 8TU. Tel. 0908-583560

Bentonite is available from all the usual pottery suppliers but as the types of Bentonite available are continually changing it is advisable to write to the individual companies for information.

US Suppliers

American Art Clay Co. Inc., (AMACO) 4717 W. 16th St., Indianapolis, IN 46222

Arch T. Flower Co. Queen St. & Ivy Hill Rd., Philadelphia, PA 19118

Bog Town Clay, 75-J Mendel Ave., S.W. Atlanta, GA 30336

Castle Clay Products, 1055 S. Fox St., Denver, CO 80223

Cedar Heights Clay Co., 50 Portsmouth Road, Oak Hill, OH 45656

Ceramic Store, 706 Richmond, Houston, TX 77006

Clay Art Center, 40 Beech St., Port Chester, NY 10573

Cole Ceramics Labs, North Eastern Office, Box 248, Sharon, CN 06069

Creek Turn Pottery Supply, Route 38, Hainesport, NJ 08036

Eagle Ceramics, 12266 Wilkins Ave., Rockville, MD 20852 and 1300 W. 9th St., Cleveland, OH 44113

Edgar Plastic Kaolin Co., Edgar, Putnam Co., FL 32049

George Fetzer Ceramic Supplies, 1205 17th Ave., Columbus, OH 43211

Georgia Kaolin Co., 433 N. Broad St., Elizabeth, NJ 07207

Hammill & Gillespie, Box 104, Livingston, NJ 07039

Kick Wheel, 802 Miami Circle N.E., Atlanta, GA 30324

L & R Specialties, 202 E. Mt. Vernon, P.O. Box 309, Nixa, MT 65714

Leslie Ceramics Supply Co., 1212 San Pablo Ave., Berkeley, CA 94706

Metropolitan Refractories, Tidewater Terminal, So. Kearny, NJ 07032

Minnesota Clay Co., 8001 Grand Ave. S., Bloomington, MN 55420

Newton Potters Supply, Inc., 96 Rumford Ave., Newton, MA 02165

Paramount, P.O. Box 463, 220 N. State St., Fairmount, MN 56031

Rovin Ceramics, 6912 Schaefer Rd., Dearborn, MI 48216

The Salem Craftsmen's Guild, 3 Alvin Pl., Upper Montclair, NJ 07043 and 1042 Salem Rd., Union, NJ 07083

Sculpture House, 38 E. 30th St., New York, NY 10016

Standard Ceramic Supply Co., Box 4435, Pittsburgh, PA 15205

Trinity Ceramic Supply Co., 9016 Diplomacy Row, Dallas, TX 75235

Western Ceramic Supply, 1601 Howard St., San Francisco, CA 94103

Westwood Ceramic Supply Co., 14400 Lomitas Ave., City of Industry, CA 91744

Jack D. Wolfe Co., 724 Meeker Ave., Brooklyn, NY 11222

Appendix 2 Bibliography

Bertel Bager: *Nature as Designer* (Frederick Warne & Co, London, 1967)

Paulus Berensohn: *Finding One's Way with Clay* (Simon & Schuster, New York; Pitman, London 1975) This book is now out of print.

Audrey Blackman: *Rolled Pottery Figures* (Pitman, London, 1978; Watson-Guptill, New York, 1979)

Michael Cardew: *Pioneer Pottery* (Longman, Harlow, Essex, 1969; St. Martin's Press, New York, 1971)

A. E. Dodd: *Dictionary of Ceramics* (Littlefield, New Jersey, 1964; George Newnes, London, 1967)

Robert Fournier: *Illustrated Dictionary of Practical Pottery* (Van Nostrand Reinhold, 1973)

Joseph Grebanier: *Chinese Stoneware Glazes* (Watson-Guptill, New York, 1975; Pitman, London, 1975)

Frank Hamer: *The Potter's Dictionary of Materials and Techniques* (Pitman, London, 1975; Watson-Guptill, New York, 1975)

Bernard Leach: *A Potter's Book* (Faber & Faber, London, 1945; Transatlantic, New York, 1973)

C. W. Parmelee: *Ceramic Glazes* (Chicago Industrial Publications, 1948)

John Reeve: *Notes on Porcelain* (*Pottery Quarterly Review*, Nos. 43 and 44)

Daniel Rhodes: *Clay and Glazes for the Potter* (Chilton, Philadelphia, 1959; Pitman, London, 1962)

Daniel Rhodes: *Stoneware and Porcelain* (Chilton, Philadelphia, 1959; Pitman, London, 1960)

Ernst Rosenthal: *Pottery and Ceramics* (Penguin, London, 1949)

D. G. A. Whitten with J. R. V. Brooks: *The Penguin Dictionary of Geology* (Penguin, London, 1972)

Nigel Wood: *Chinese Porcelain* (*Pottery Quarterly Review*, No. 47)

Nigel Wood: *Oriental Glazes* (Pitman, London, 1978; Watson-Guptill, New York, 1978)

W. E. Worrall: *Clays, their Nature, Origin and General Properties* (Maclaren & Sons, London, 1964; Transatlantic, New York, 1968)

W. E. Worrall: *Raw Materials* (Maclaren & Sons, London, 1964)

The Story of China Clay (English China Clays Ltd)

Molochite (English China Clays Ltd).

Index